Ultimate
Snowboarding

This is a Carlton Book

This edition published in 1998

"Good Friday" originally appeared on the Snowboarding On-Line website [SOL] in April, 1996.

"Surfing The Slopes" originally appeared in the United Airlines in-flight magazine *Hemispheres* in December, 1996.

"The Tao of Physics, the Point of Diminishing Returns, And The Man Who Didn't Want A Million Dollars" originally appeared in the October, 1995 issue of *Snowboarder Magazine.*

"Fear of Alaska?" is a combination of two stories originally appearing in *Snowboarder Magazine* – "What Are You Afraid Of?", December, 1997, and "Prey Hard", October, 1996.

"Tom Burt Interview" originally appeared in the February 1997 issue of *TransWorld SNOWboarding Magazine.*

"Contests are Back!" originally appeared in the March, 1995 issue of *TransWorld SNOWboarding Magazine.*

"At Home With the World's Greatest Snowboarder" originally appeared in the September, 1996 issue of *Snowboarder Magazine.*

"Snowboarding's Timeline" originally appeared in *TransWorld SNOWboarding Business*, and was compiled as "It All Started When?" in a promotional industry planner printed by TransWorld Media.

"When Man Made Mountains" originally appeared as an essay on man-made snowboarding environments in the October, 1994 issue of *Snowboarder Magazine.*

Portions of the Ross Rebagliati interview originally appeared on the website twsnow.com and in the October 1998 issue of *TransWorld SNOWboarding.*

Portions of the Michele Taggart interview originally appeared in the January 1996 issue of *TransWorld SNOWboarding.*

Design © Carlton Books Limited 1998

A CIP catalogue record for this book is available from the British Library.

Hardback: ISBN 1 85868 554 0
Paperback: ISBN 1 85868 513 3

Project Manager: Julian Flanders
Project Editor: Tim Dedopulos
Senior Art Editor: Zoë Maggs
Designer: Simon Mercer
Production: Garry Lewis

Printed and bound in Dubai

About the Contributors

Billy Miller, the Editor of the book, is a journalist for *Transworld Snowboarding* the biggest selling snowboarding magazine in the US. He is based in Oceanside, California. He has assembled a team of expert writers and boarders to compile *Ultimate Snowboarding*.

Mikey Franco started snowboarding while employed as a ticket checker at Blue Knob, Pennsylvania. They didn't allow the sport, so on his third offense he was fired. In 1988 he began to teach snowboarding at Tussey Mountain, Pennsylvania, and in 1990 moved to Jackson Hole. He became a DECL Examiner for the American Association of Snowboard Instructors in 1996.

Besides her past roles as MTV veejay and Winter Olympic commentator, **Kennedy** is a larger-than-real-life personality. Currently, she's finishing up her first book, entitled *Hey, Ladies!*

Matthew Linnell is a juggler, former pro snowboarder and made his own snowboarding video, *Neato*. He has a degree in film and literature from the University of Santa Cruz.

Jeff Galbraith is snowboarding royalty (his grandfather Jack was mountain manager/part owner of Alpental, Washington). As talented a writer as he is a skeptic, this senior editor of *Snowboarder Magazine* has work that's appeared in *International Snowboard Magazine, Powder, Time* and *Jim.*

John Erben lives on a boat at the bottom of an avalanche path in Rain, Alaska.

Eric Blehm is the former editor of *TransWorld SNOWboarding Magazine* and has travelled the world writing for various publications including *Powder, Outside, Adventure West* and *Playboy.*

Affectionately christened 'The Man Who Knew Too Much', **Lee Crane** is a snowboard media pioneer. *TransWorld SNOWboarding's* first managing editor, a successful freelance journalist, respected TV commentator and founder of the superlative website Snowboarding On-Line (SOL), he's currently Webmaster for TransWorld Media.

Snowboarding renaissance man **Brad Steward** has had his fingers in every corner of the sport. A salesperson, photographer, writer, filmer, designer, executive and rider for almost two decades, he is one of the founders and the president of Bonfire snowboard clothing.

Jamie Meiselman has been managing editor of both *TransWORLD SNOWboarding* and *TransWorld SNOWboarding Business*, and is now general manager of Blax/Generics USA. A rider for some 19 years, he engineered some of the first step-in boot/bindings.

Ross Rebagliati from Whistler, British Columbia is the Olympic Gold Medalist in snowboard Giant Slalom. With first-place finishes at the legendary Mt. Baker Banked Slalom and the U.S. Open Super-G too, he's the most well-rounded snowboard race champion in the world.

Eric Wright spent his formative snowboarding years in Jackson Hole, Wyoming where he was responsible for the oft-imitated 'zine *Hard Pipe*. Now a field editor for *TransWorld SNOWboarding*, he's still as hardcore as the day is long.

Ultimate
Snowboarding

The all-action guide to the world's most exciting sport

EDITOR:

BILLY MILLER

CARLTON

Contents

Introduction

Snowboarding is freeriding – the ultimate fusion of sporting fun and self-expression. Guided by some of the sharpest voices in the business, this book will give you an encyclopedic look at the activity as a whole. The book covers everything from snowboarding's historical roots, through where it's coming from, to board design and how to select the best equipment. Techniques show the reader how to do it, how to get tricky with it, and what a pro's life is like. Other sections look at its evolution, discover what makes those hard-booters such fanatics, and check out to the competition and the culture; and feature candid interviews with the sport's brightest stars. Yet trying to take some all-encompassing meaning from all that could prove as futile as predicting where snowboarding may go next. To some, it is a mere leisure activity; to others, something worth devoting your life to. Now, courtesy of the XVIIIth Winter Olympics, snowboarding is a fast-growing sport married to the mainstream forever.

Made up, as it is, of so many individuals influenced by the infinite directions you can surf down a slope, snowboarding ultimately has as many meanings as there are people pursuing it – uniting us with snow-slathered mountains in singularly carved lines of love, the essence of which each must divine unto themselves.

Good Friday

Lost?
Snowboarding fun can be found.

"I know it's around here... maybe down by that sign," says Jew, after interminable rounds of pinball down at the Rat.

All I knew was that the first warming of spring was in the air, the corn was still soft and that resort lifts closed too early.

Mount Hood Meadows resort was shut and we were driving back to Friday beers in Government Camp, Oregon with the rest of the monkeys. Suddenly Jew veered towards the hard shoulder. "Wait a minute, we could hike the pipe at Timberline! Then it's a full moon tonight – so after, we could take the trail that leads you all the way back into Govie, to the back door of the Rat practically! I am not exactly sure about the line... but if it's soft, it could be *guh-uuhd*!"

He looks at me sideways, which always means I either have no reason, or every reason, to worry.

"How's the pipe?" Jew asks Euro Eric on our way through Govie.

"Pipe sucks," says Eric in a thick accent, backed up by his bro halfway through his beer. "It hasn't been cut in a few weeks. Nobody's worked on it, nobody's shaped it. It could be good. It's

warm enough. But nobody's done anything to it at all."

Jew and I look at each other. That wasn't the news we were waiting to hear but

we're going anyway. It's too early to burn out on a bar stool. Too light to quit just yet.

"Got to be careful to stay out of this stuff on the way back," says Jew, looking down to our thick footfalls in the freshly tilled corn. "There's nothing cat drivers hate worse that some yahoo ruining something they just finished."

"They might run us over," I say, shivering with the thought of a few summers back when a snowcat's brake slipped; it rolled over and killed some pipeside-sitting girl. That deterrent is keeping me the hell away from anyone's labored rows of Etch-A-Sketch.

I don't even ask the cat drivers where the halfpipe is when they zip by. Jew wants me to, but I figure they wouldn't share the joy with a couple of un-ticketed, off-hours kooks. Just the threat of their program fucked-up would be enough to chase us off.

MADNESS – NO, JUST SNOWBOARDING.

YOU'VE HAD THE LESSON – NOW JUST PROVE IT ...

IN THE MIDDLE OF NOWHERE.

If they did, I imagined smearing huge, spiteful 'S's down their precision drudgery ...

"... I don't know if we should keep going over, go down to that sign, or keep going up so we can get a better look. Eric said it was right by the lift ... ?" Jew breaks my sedation and I notice much of our earlier chutzpah drying up. Not surprising, we are seemingly in the middle of nowhere, trudging out into the white mire with the goal nowhere in sight. This strikes me as ridiculous, though not altogether bad.

Hiking up to a higher vantage it's still a

mystery. Finally, while I play around a lift ramp Jew bravely inquires of one of the cat drivers. I expect to be escorted off the hill by a grooming blade, but they tell him where it's at before zipping off to their business. "See! I told you it was by that sign!", he says with the certainty of hindsight.

We buckle in to our boards and roll through lumpy mounds in the unshaped snowboard park before finally locating the halfpipe. It looks forgotten, not even cut the whole way down. Walls at decent size, but unsculpted and partially melted. Sucking, in fact, as reported.

"This looks okay! A two-hitter maybe," chirps Jew, dropping in.

Finding the line is a struggle. The walls are soft and hittable, but it takes much labor to get out even three times. Jeff is the right hand of Tim Windell's snowboard camps and has much pipe experience.

"I blow a grab, bounce backwards off the lip and flop to the flat bottom on my ass."
Billy Miller

He shows me how to roll in at an angle off the wall and pump down the tranny instead of blowing all your speed in the flat. He can spin a 540 degrees with only a smidgen of clearance off the lip.

Jew is also experienced in having fun; in gabbing about whatever; in analyzing the minutiae of technical freestyle, and in laughing with me instead of at me as I blow a grab, bounce backwards off the lip and flop to the flat bottom on my ass.

We took turns hiking that two-hit line (three if you really milked it) while the sun lazily sank in the west and the valley pollu-

tion was backlit with a warm, pink glow. We didn't talk a whole lot, concentrating on saving our dwindling strength for another shot at a day's personal best.

I could brag it was the most epic session ever. I could say we stayed there until the full moon hovered overhead, then rode that secret trail all the way back to Govie to shit-talk the story 10 times bigger and better.

The truth is, it wasn't long before a day's exertion produced weak limbs and pits in our stomachs. We listened to the birds hidden in the trees, harbingers of the predicted early spring. It may not have been the most epic session ever, but just being out there was *good*. Even though the winter had gone too fast there were many blistering days of soft, sweet corn kickers yet to be reaped.

"It was a good day," says Jew, while we eat Frosted Mini-Wheats from the box to combat low blood-sugar shakes, rolling in his van back down the hill. "And nobody told me to have a good day either. You know what I mean? You know how you can be having the suckingest day ever and everyone keeps telling you, 'Have a good da-aay! Have a good da-aay!' This was one of those days where I went out and made it a good day and had a good day but not one person *told me* I had to have one, you know what I'm saying? One hell of a good day!

"Hey, what are you doing this weekend? What are you doing for Easter?"

Editor Billy Miller

HAVING A COOL TIME.

By Eric Blehm

Carving a niche

Discounted as a fad a decade ago, snowboarding now appeals to adventurous spirits of all ages.

 chapter 1

SNOWBOARDERS EVEN OUTNUMBER SKIERS ON
SOME MOUTNAINS.

he middle-aged woman was muttering the numbers under her breath, loud enough for me to hear, "44, 45, 46 ... " When her eyes met mine she glanced down at my snowboard, and said, "47." Smiling politely, she turned back around so she was facing forward in the lift line. It was a quad-chair and I was single, so I tapped her on the shoulder.

"Just two of you?" I asked, motioning toward her and a man who appeared to be her husband. A minute later, as we were being whisked up the mountain, I asked, "Were you counting snowboarders back there?" Without hesitation the gentleman returned, "Yes, they, err, you people make up nearly half the folks on the hill today. Where'd you all come from?"

For some staunch traditionalists, snowboarders have come straight out of their worst nightmares – the bad boys and girls of winter who, according to a 1994 television episode of *American Journal*, 'Are knocking down skiers like bowling pins.' Ironically that same year, the May Fifth cover of *The Wall Street Journal* proclaimed: 'Snowboarding Scores as the Fastest Growing Sport – with participation up 50 per cent since the previous winter.'

Appropriately, a day later, Ride Snowboards became the first snowboard-specific company to go public. It raised over $5.75 million its first day on the New York Stock Exchange.

All this from a sport that was once discounted as a fad by many ski resorts and mainstream media journalists. *Parade Magazine* quoted *Time* in its January 1988 issue, calling snowboarding the 'Worst New Sport.' To traditionalists, the breezy fad is a clumsy intrusion on the sleek precision of downhill skiing, but to some 100,000 enthusiasts, many of them adolescent males, it is the coolest snow sport of the season ... Of course, there are holdouts. Complains veteran Vermont skier Mary Simons: "Snowboarding is not about grace and style, but about raging hormones."

But raging hormones were the last thing I felt when I waved good-bye to the friendly couple and started carving turns down the groomed corduroy of Mammoth Mountain's High Sierra slopes – the same magical California Range of Light that so captivated naturalist John Muir. He once

wrote, "The mountains are calling me, and I must go."

Thanks to snowboarding, increasing numbers of once winter-averse surfers, skateboarders and other colorful flatlanders are also being called to the mountains. And with them, growth and excitement is returning to a flat ski market. The National Sporting Goods Association says participation in Alpine skiing in the United States declined from an estimated 12.4 million in 1988 to just 10.6 million in 1994. The number of snowboarders has increased from 1.3 million in 1988 to 2.1 million in 1994 – a number that could grow to almost 5 million by 2000.

The halfpipe

I linked turns for 100 yards and turned on to another run designated as a snowboard park, where quarterpipes and tabletop jumps have been built to provide an arena for riders to practice tricks. Many of these have actually been borrowed from skateboard halfpipe riding.

It is quite appropriate that, in fact, the snow halfpipe that has been the sport's main draw for media attention and youthful riders.

The technical equivalent of gymnastics, diving or freestyle skiing, halfpipe riding captures the spirit of snowboarding with a no-holds-barred attitude of spinning, flipping and jumping from one vertical wall of the halfpipe to the next. These are personal expression sessions where riders sometimes go forward and other times go fakie (backward), a technique that is very difficult to master.

Flashing by on my left, Mammoth Mountain's snowboard team coach Dan Large was setting gates for his racers who were training in earnest for a slot on the team to represent the United States at the XVIII Olympic Games in Nagano, Japan, where snowboarding was to make its

WITH THE AID OF TABLETOP JUMPS AERIAL TRICKS ARE EASY.

debut as a full-fledged sport. The final US team Olympic qualifier was held right here in Mammoth, where the announcement of the team was also made.

The first board

Snowboarding has come a long way since the creation of the first board in 1965. On Christmas morning, Sherman Poppen – an inventor with several industrial patents under his belt – walked outside his home in Muskegon, Michigan, looked at a snow-covered hill and saw a wave.

Poppen had always been fascinated by surfing but lived far from the ocean. Remembering his daughter Wendy's past attempts at standing up on her sled, he screwed two pairs of children's skis together and fashioned a surfboard for the snow. Within a few days, all the neighborhood kids were begging Mr Poppen for what Mrs Poppen dubbed the 'Snurfer', a mix of 'snow' and 'surfer.'

Six months later, Poppen licensed the idea to sporting goods company Brunswick and over the next 10 years, upwards of a million Snurfers were produced and sold.

"The Snurfer marks the start of the onslaught." Eric Blehm

As with all inventions, there is speculation as to who made the first true snowboard. Tom Sims, owner of Sims Snowboards located in Seattle, Washington claims to have made the first 'ski-board' for an eight-grade project in 1963. But, as far as bringing the idea to the masses, Poppen's Snurfer marks the start of the onslaught.

Jake Burton Carpenter, founder of Burton snowboards – the largest snowboard brand in the world – credits the Snurfer as his ride, as does Demetrije Milovich, who started Winterstick snowboards, and Chris Sanders who founded Avalanche snowboards.

Quickly, the US-born sport filtered throughout Europe, with early pioneers such as Frenchman Régis Rolland riding his swallowtail snowboard into history as the 'good guy snowboarder' being pursued by 'bad guy skiers' in the cult movies known simply as *Apocalypse Snow I, II* and *III*.

British agent James Bond provided mass appeal for the sport when he escaped capture by snowboarding away in the 1985 release of *A View to a Kill*.

WHERE STICKS ONCE LIVED SNOWBOARDS NOW SIT.

American snowboarders Steve Link and Tom Sims doubled for 007 on location in Iceland and the Swiss Alps.

Still, the sport was struggling for acceptance at more than 75 per cent of the 'ski' resorts worldwide. The average snowboarder was an adolescent male with an attitude and lifestyle meshed with urban skateboarding and surfing, which didn't set too well with resort management.

Mass appeal

Only a few idiots were to blame for cutting lift lines, riding out of control and disregarding boundaries, but the sport was stereotyped and anyone on a board was pegged as 'one to watch' by ski patrols and 'one to watch out for' by skiers.

Riders started to police each other and write letters to the resorts, lobbying for acceptance. In many cases, snowboarders were given the opportunity to demonstrate their proficiency but were still banned. Today, the last holdouts are few: Alta and Deer Valley, Utah; Taos in New Mexico and Mad River Glen in Vermont are among the few 'skiing only' mountains left in the United States. Utah's Park City finally gave in, ironically, *after* it bid for the snowboard events at the 2002 Winter Olympics.

In fact, snowboarding is reaching critical mass. Resorts that banned the sport a decade ago are now providing extras to attract its participants. Flat areas are highlighted on trail maps to warn riders to keep their speed up, and many resorts offer terrain parks and halfpipes so riders have a place to hang out. Usually skiers and riders get along fine. Snowboarding is increasingly a sport for adults and families, ranging from toddlers to geriatrics, just like skiing.

Just like the hot dog skiers in the seventies, riders have become the new gypsies of the world, sleeping on couches and scraping up money for lift tickets.

SNOWBOARDS LINED UP FOR THE NEXT DAY.

"Industry sources estimate that the sale of snowboards and related equipment could reach more than $150 million by 1997-1998."
Dain Bosworth

The hard core have put college on hold to be bums in the mountain towns of the world, harboring hopes of becoming the next superstars. With big-name corporations such as Pepsi and Nike vying to associate their names with the sport, can you blame them? Huge sponsor salaries aren't uncommon for snowboarders, some of whom still can't legally buy a beer.

World's worst-kept secret

It's safe to say that snowboarding isn't a fad anymore. A snowboard industry report compiled and researched by Dain Bosworth, a member of the New York Stock Exchange, says, 'Industry sources estimate that the sale of snowboards and related equipment could reach more than $150 million in annual sales in the United States by 1997-98, or approximately one-half as large as the current US Alpine skiing market.'

As I rode away from the park, I got into a rhythm laying over my carves. I veered off the trail into the trees and found myself in a spectacular glade of untracked powder. My first turns threw spray into the wind and, as icy crystals showered my face, I guided my board between the snow-laden pines.

Jumping back in the lift line for another run, I saw the skiing couple I'd chatted with entering the lodge. It dawned on me that I'd shamelessly tried to sell them on the sport. Then I understood why a friend of mine described the snowboarding explosion as the world's worst-kept secret – you can't help but

HAVE SNOWBOARD, WILL TRAVEL.

IT'S EASY WHEN YOU KNOW HOW.

Equipment
in brief

By Eric Blehm

Buying a board

The cost of snowboard equipment is similar to that of Alpine skiing. A brand new snowboard with bindings retails for anywhere from $350 to $600. Snowboard boots can range from $90 to $300.

It's a good idea to try before you buy. Many shops offer demo programs where you can sample a few boards and then deduct the demo price from your final purchase.

THERE ARE MANY BOARDS ON OFFER.

Lift tickets

On the hill, lift tickets range from $20 at some smaller resorts to as much as $50 at large destination resorts.

Board rentals

Snowboard rentals are available at virtually every resort and many ski and snowboard shops. Prices range from $20 to $35 for a full-day boot, board & binding combo. Soft boot versions – as opposed to the ones that are hard and ski boot-like – are more forgiving when you're a beginner and generally they are more comfortable on your feet. The availability of step-in boots and bindings has made the adaptation process easier than ever.

Lessons

As with skiing, it's highly recommended you tackle the sport under the guidance of an instructor. Virtually every ski resort now offers lessons as part of their 'ski' school.

What kind and size of board should I ride?

A fool-proof answer to your pressing questions.

By Jamie Meiselman

As much as magazines, catalogues and advertisements state that this year's snowboards are 'vastly improved' over last year's models, the method of properly fitting a snowboarder to his or her favourite stick remains refreshingly constant.

For a snowboard is simply a well-trimmed sandwich of wood, fiberglass, steel and other materials. It doesn't know or care whether you are male, female, blond or brunette, French or Finnish. A snowboard only reacts to what it can feel: the snow below it and your weight and feet above it.

Knowing this less-than-sexy truth, designers build boards around three variables: terrain preference, which determines the board shape or outline; foot size, which determines its width; and rider weight, which then decides the length and flex pattern of the board.

The formula is simple enough, but it is amazing when you realise just how many riders are on snowboards that are painfully unsuited to their needs and physical dimensions.

Boardfinder system

Boardfinder system was designed to put a serious dent in mismatch misery. It takes your vital statistics and riding preferences and turns them into a perfectly-matched snowboard.

If more people took the 'finder's advice, and not the neighbor's son's – who's a 'black diamond rider' – the snowboarding world would be a happier place. Please play your part…

Freestyle/Freeride Boardfinder – higher slopes

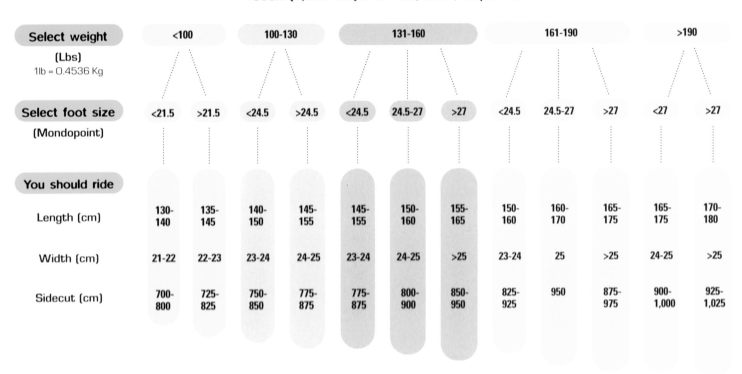

Select terrain

Big mountains

>500m (1,500 foot) of vertical, softer, deeper snow

Select weight (Lbs) 1lb = 0.4536 Kg	<100		100-130		131-160			161-190			>190	
Select foot size (Mondopoint)	<21.5	>21.5	<24.5	>24.5	<24.5	24.5-27	>27	<24.5	24.5-27	>27	<27	>27
You should ride												
Length (cm)	130-140	135-145	140-150	145-155	145-155	150-160	155-165	150-160	160-170	165-175	165-175	170-180
Width (cm)	21-22	22-23	23-24	24-25	23-24	24-25	>25	23-24	25	>25	24-25	>25
Sidecut (cm)	700-800	725-825	750-850	775-875	775-875	800-900	850-950	825-925	950	875-975	900-1,000	925-1,025

Freestyle/Freeride Boardfinder – lower slopes

Select terrain

Small mountains

<500m (1,500 foot) of vertical, icier, thinner snow

Select weight (Lbs) — 1lb = 0.4536 Kg

	<100		100-130		131-160			161-190			>190	
Select foot size (Mondopoint)	<21.5	>21.5	<24.5	>24.5	<24.5	24.5-27	>27	<24.5	24.5-27	>27	<27	>27
You should ride												
Length (cm)	125-135	130-140	135-145	140-150	140-150	145-155	150-160	145-155	150-160	150-160	155-165	155-165
Width (cm)	21-22	22-23	23-24	24-25	23-24	24-25	>25	23-24	24-25	>25	24-25	>25
Sidecut (cm)	650-700	675-775	675-775	725-825	725-825	750-850	800-900	775-875	800-900	800-900	850-950	850-950

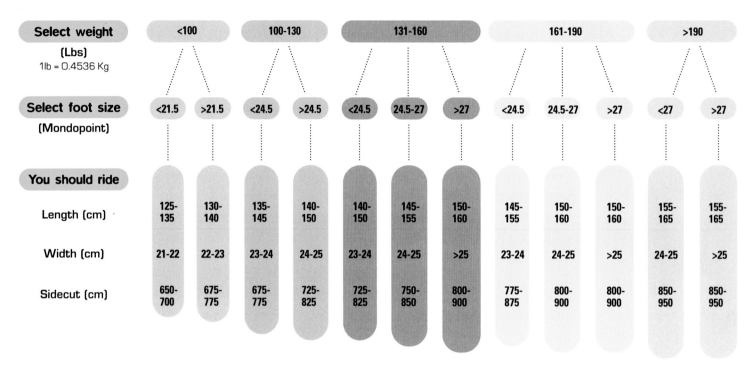

Freecarve Boardfinder

Select weight (Lbs) — 1lb = 0.4536 Kg

	<140		140-180		>180	
Select Turn Radius Preferemce	Small Slalom	Large GS	Small Slalom	Large GS	Small Slalom	Large GS
Select Board						
Length (cm)	140-150	150-160	150-160	160-170	155-165	150-160
Width (cm)	18-20	18-20	19-21	19-21	20-22	20-22
Sidecut (cm)	800-900	900-1000	850-950	1000-1200	800-900	1100-1300

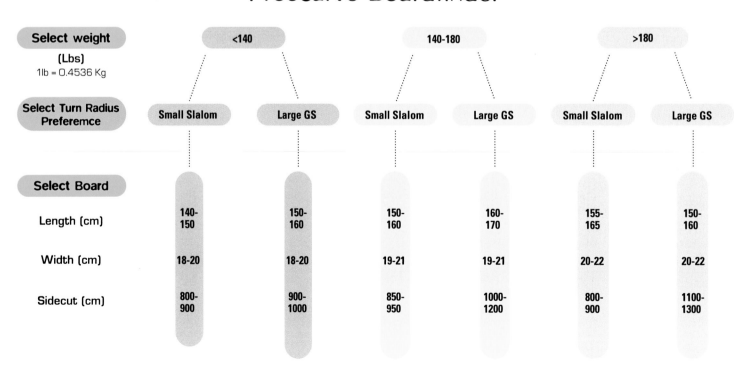

Boot/Binding finding

Your step in the right direction
By Jamie Meiselman

Since the step-in binding explosion in 1995, your choice of boots/bindings has grown exponentially – more types, endless companies, precious little standardization. An easy-to-comprehend guide to choosing the right set-up has become more necessary than ever.

Getting the best boots and bindings for your needs is more involved than answering general questions and following a simple flow chart. You need an understanding of the systems out there and what type of riding they're for.

Unlike buying boards, the nice thing about buying boots and bindings is you can try them on for fit and function in the showroom. With step-ins, make sure you're comfortable stepping in and out at the shop. It will be harder on the hill when snow and slippery slopes come into play.

If a boot hurts, or the heel lifts when you strap in on the carpet, chances are it

A BAD BOOT AND BINDING CHOICE WILL GIVE YOU HELL, SO CHOOSE RIGHT.

will be worse on the snow – whatever the salesperson tells you.

The types

There are three categories of boot/binding:
1. Soft systems
2. Step-In systems
3. Hard systems

Each channels the rider's energy differently to the board, so each feels different. We can explain how each one works and what kind of rider it suits, and you can decide what riding style you're after.

Soft

Traditional soft boots and bindings rely on the binding straps and the binding highback for retaining the boot and providing control of the board. This is generally the most flexible of the different types. Because the binding is providing most of the support, the boot has a softer sole and can roll slightly from side-to-side within the binding. As it has the most margin for error, it is also the least responsive of the three. Many top technical freestyle riders prefer the soft system because there's a better chance of recovering sketchy landings. Soft boots are also comfortable for hiking and walking around in.

Step-In

A new and welcome addition to the snowboard world, step-ins have brought more than just an easy way of getting in and out to the table. In place of the traditional bindings, the sole of the boot is stiffened and attached to the binding with some kind of latching. This stops the boot rolling in the binding, providing more response, but also less margin of error than you get with a soft system. Generally, the stiffer sole also means quicker edge-to-edge response than with the traditional soft type.

For its performance advantage, the step-in has quickly become the choice of

GETTING THE RIGHT BOOTS IS THE FIRST STEP.

many top freeriders. For its convenience, it is also a top choice for rentals and beginners and intermediate riders.

Hard

The hard system is the opposite of the soft system in that it relies entirely on the structure of the boot to control the board. Hard boots have a stiff, plastic shell, so they are the most precise of the different types. It is for this reason that they are, generally, used by carvers and racers, who want the most instant, precise control over the boards possible.

Within the hard system, there are both traditional toe-clips and step-ins systems. Generally, a step-in is slightly stiffer than toe-clips, because step-ins use an interlocking latch mechanism to secure the boot to the binding. The latch allows minimal movement of the boot within the binding, while toe-clips allow the boot a degree of roll within the binding.

Okay, so now what?

Decide in which of the three directions you wish to go. Read the explanations and see which 'bottom line rider' you best identify with.

Soft system sub-categories

Freestyle boots

These boots are relatively soft flexing forward and side-to-side. They also have a softer sole allowing unimpeded contact with the board/binding underfoot. Freestyle soft boots are generally used by riders on smaller mountains who do smaller jumps and put less stress on the ankle and foot. Some top riders are shunning soft 'freestyle' boots because they need more support for landing really, really, really high airs in the pipe or snowboard park.

Bottom line rider: technical freestyle rider who rides at small mountains or doesn't get huge air.

Freeride boots

Freeride boots are generally stiffer flexing forward and side-to-side, for support and response at higher speeds and bigger air. These stiffer boots are most common on larger mountain ranges and with professional freestyle riders who need more ankle support to land big drops and airs.

Bottom line rider: technical freestyle rider who rides big mountains or goes big.

Freestyle bindings

Usually referred to as 'two-strap' high-

backs, these allow a good degree of boot roll within the binding, but provide steady heel-hold for toeside response and a relatively stiff highback for heelside response. As the demands of freestyle riders rise over the years, highbacks have become higher and stiffer to provide enough support.

Bottom line rider: any freestyle/freerider who uses soft boots.

Freeride bindings

Rarely sighted on slopes any more due to the advent of step-ins, freeride soft bindings usually have a third shin-strap for extra support on toeside turns and less side-to-side roll of the boot and ankle. They perform similarly to a hard system, but because of the inconvenience of three straps, most riders who want this performance level will go with stiff step-in or hard systems.

Bottom line rider: freeriders who want to have some extra toeside support but don't want to step-in.

Step-in system sub-categories

Internal or pivoting highback

Step-in boots with an internal or pivoting highback are the most supportive of the step-ins. The highback is on some type of pivot point which, by following the leg movements, gives positive heelside support through the entire turn. This constant support makes pivoting-highback boots best suited for all-mountain freeriding.

Bottom line rider: A freerider wanting maximum heelside support who doesn't do many big airs.

External static highback

Several step-in boots have a static highback on the outside of the rear of the boot, which mimics the feel of a soft binding and allows more margin of error than an inter-

nal or pivoting highback. This makes them better suited for freestyle riding and jumping. The stiff sole gives an improvement edge-to-edge quickness over traditional soft boots and bindings.

Bottom line rider: freestyle/Freeriders who jump; Beginner/intermediate all-mountain riders.

Highback on binding

A third class of step-in puts the highback on the binding itself. Performance is similar to that of an external static highback, but with a highback on the binding, stepping in can become more awkward. Without a built-in highback, the boots are lighter and more comfortable for hiking. These step-ins are probably the closest in feel and performance to soft bindings, and that makes them a good choice for technical freestyle riders who choose to step in.

Bottom line rider: technical freestyle riders who do a lot of hiking and want quicker response.

Hard system sub-categories

Freecarve boots

Freecarve hard boots have a relatively soft plastic shell with plenty of response and a bit of flexibility for comfort. The flex allows a margin for error in chattery conditions and comfort when riding powder or softer

GET YOUR BOOT
AND BINDING
COMBINATION
RIGHT FOR
MAXIUM EFFECT.

snow. This style of riding is popular in Europe, where many riders prefer to ride the long, groomed runs there with a much more supportive setup.

Bottom line rider: carvers who ride some powder and ungroomed slopes.

Freecarve bindings

Freecarving plate bindings mirror the boots with more side-to-side flex than a racing binding. Slight inward, i.e. knee-to-knee flex in the bindings allows the rider to absorb vibration and make any necessary adjustments in choppy snow.

Bottom line rider: carvers who ride some powder and ungroomed slopes.

Race boots

Race boots are essentially very stiff. In all directions. This allows instant power transmission and minimal margin of error. These boots work best at high speeds on groomed slopes or race courses and should not be used for anything else.

Bottom line rider: racers or very aggressive freecarvers who are only going to ride on hardpacked slopes.

Race bindings

Racing plate bindings also allow little margin of error. Built with a very stiff baseplate, usually of aluminum or carbon fiber, the result is like bolting your boots to the board. The boots have minimal play within the binding and movements are instantly transferred from boot to board.

Bottom line rider: racers or very aggressive freecarvers who are only going to ride on hardpacked slopes.

Dress rehearsal

Snowboard clothing goes on one leg, or sleeve, at a time.
By Brad Steward

Someone is staring at your pants. Not because the pants are neon-green fleece and feature bright-blue suspenders that crawl over your shoulder in an unidentifiable maze of webbing. They are staring at your pants because it is clear they don't correctly blend the fit, fabric, function and fashion of snowboard riding apparel – and if your pants fit the description above they are ugly, but that's another story.

There is one thing that sets snowboard apparel apart from every other category of outerwear – a range of features developed over time by rider-designers which experienced buyers and riders call 'snowboard specific'. The label is also a quick way to tell if what you're spending a ton of money on is what you want.

As snowboard 'fashion' ripples through the design world, many items look snowboard specific but aren't. The best snowboard-specific apparel pays special attention to the four Fs. Knowing the details will help you buy outerwear that performs and still looks good.

The four Fs

The goal of the four Fs is to avoid getting, what one might call, the fifth F! The major factor is where you're going to be riding. Then common sense and planning will help you buy what is appropriate for the conditions where you ride. For now, try to make fashion a secondary concern.

Fit

The fit of snowboard apparel is not like traditional ski wear. Take the snowboard jacket. Look in the mirror and see if the fabric is bunching or stretching – signs of a bad fit. Don't confuse 'loose' with 'bad'. Loose is comfortable, bad restricts movement and adds weight. Zip the jacket up to the collar. Does it fit around your chin? Can you move your neck without restriction? If so, that's good. With the jacket fully zipped, raise both arms above your head. If the jacket rises and exposes your waist, it isn't snowboard specific.

THERE'S MORE TO
PICKING OUTERWEAR
THAN A SENSE OF
STYLE.

I use the arms-up test to find fashion fakes and re-styled skiwear imitations. I regularly find seven out of 10 jackets will fail – even those from good snowboard brands.

For pants, the rise should allow full leg movement and not restrict the waist. Most riders like a looser waistband for easier movement. If this is your choice, make sure the pants have something that prevents snow dropping down your back. Many have expandable back panels for a loose fit and protection. If there is a staircase in the shop, ask to climb it and check the fit in motion. If the pant has suspenders, attach these while walking, also wearing your jacket and a backpack to see if the straps interfere with the comfort of a backpack. Many snowboard pants have suspenders that allow you to drop the entire back panel for pit stops at the boys' or girls' room – a great feature that is appreciated through use.

Another fit test is the cuffs. Wear your own gloves and boots with any jacket and pants you are trying. Wear them as normal. If the jacket cuff doesn't fit around or inside your glove cuff, it will leak. You can buy new gloves, but in any case, make sure you've got a seal between jacket and glove cuffs. Many snowboarders wear short, motocross-style gloves because the inner cuff of their jackets are adequate to achieve snow sealage.

If the pant bottoms do not fit over the boots, don't buy them. The pant leg cuff should slide easily over the boot top and have an inner gaiter, which is a covering from the instep to above the ankle. Many snowboard-specific pants have longer gaiters with either double grabbing elastic or a lace lock to stop the pant 'post-holing,' or climbing up your leg when you hike through deep snow. The best riding pants also have a hem protector at the base of the leg cuff, allowing you to wear your pants a little loose without ripping the bottom hem out of your pant leg.

A final fit test is on the jacket hood. With the jacket fully zipped, put the hood on with your goggles and adjust the hood to its closest-fitting position on your face. If the hood doesn't fit your face, you will get a cold draft down your back. If the hood doesn't adjust, don't buy it for riding; it's a fashion hood. The hood should allow full mobility and not be difficult to adjust in any way. Hood adjusters are best at the front of the face, not on the back of the neck, where they could hook to a chair lift and choke you. You don't have to reach around your back to adjust your hood either. The best hood adjusters are minimal ones don't flap around in the wind as you ride.

"If you're going to Alaska with no hood, you'll die." Brad Steward

Most people prefer removable hoods, which give you an option whether to use them or not – and helps shops sell them to you. Backcountry riders prefer hoods that don't come off, because they don't want the cold to come through at the back of the neck. If you are riding the pipe on sunny days, you may be able to save a few bucks by getting something without a hood. If you're going to Alaska with no hood, you'll die. The weather does whatever it wants, no matter how you are dressed.

Fabric

Any fabric that takes marketing charts, detailed tests and information is probably a waterproof-breathable material. Snow and rain hitting you on the outside will not get in, while sweat will evaporate out. This keeps you dry inside, not clammy-feeling.

Ratings and charts use one number for the amount of water the fabric allows out and another number for breathability. The breathability rating should be as high as possible, no matter what level of waterproofing you buy. Be it a coating or a laminate, a good all-around fabric falls somewhere around 8000-12,000 waterproof with a 6000 breathability rating. For

IT MAY LOOK GOOD BUT IF IT DOESN'T FIT, DON'T WEAR IT!

EVEN IF YOU DON'T DRESS TO IMPRESS, THERE ARE OTHER WAYS OF LOOKING GOOD IN SNOWBOARDING.

more technical environments a 20,000 waterproof is the standard. For summer camps and warm-weather riding, a 6000-8000 waterproof should suffice. In all cases, the breathability rating should always be around 6000.

Function

Function is the variable element in your buying decision, based on layering. The first layer is usually the long underwear worn next to your skin, which gets sweat away from your body as quickly as possible. The second layer, comprised of a wide range of materials, keeps the sweat going out and insulates you. The third layer, your jacket and pant, is your protection.

There is more complex layering, but if you address these three layers, then you will find that you are pretty comfortable in most riding situations.

To evaluate whether function is a gimmick or a benefit, you have to know where you are riding and what your needs are.

Make a list of the benefits you want from your clothing. For example:

"I want to be warm, on very cold days; dry, even when it's snowing hard; wear my jacket to work; ride my mountain bike in my jacket; and my butt to stay warm."

Now a salesperson can guide me to jackets and pants that are highly waterproof and breathable and introduce me to layering. If I say I want to ride my mountain bike in my jacket, a good salesperson will know the solution is a lightweight shell with a removable insulating liner.

You may have to teach your salesperson to think this way.

If you ask for a pant that is warm and dry you may decide on a certain type of fabric used exclusively on snow. For your jacket, you may want a fabric that you can also wear on the street.

Focusing on function in place of features allows you to see the forest for the trees and forces the salesperson to give your purchase some thought.

Fashion

The final F is the toughest of all – fashion is really a moving target where there are no rules. Snow-boarding is like anything pre-teen. When it falls in love with something it really goes all out!

When neon was happening in the early 80s, snowboarding had it bad. When race styles and stripes came in, snowboarding, like some dumb kid finding its way in the world, fell head over heels.

The best way to look at fashion is to stay focused on what you need, then follow your style instincts. The mountain doesn't care if you look cool or authentic. If you are a fashion victim and have horrible taste, odds are you're the last to know, so don't sweat it too hard.

Shop around and gather as much detail as you can. Check warranties and the shop's service record so you avoid that nasty little fifth F. Most importnatly, spend tons of money, so that people like me never have to get a real job!

A ticket...
to ride

By Mikey Franco

The supervisor at Jackson Hole, Wyoming Snowboard
gives us the first lesson in snowboarding.

remember when I saw my first snowboard. I was 14 and didn't have much money, but I had to have it. So, after saving and saving, there was enough money in the piggy bank – and it was mine! I didn't think about how I would get down the hill, nor did I care. I just wanted to ride. I had been skiing for about one season (actually 30 days of an east coast winter). That should be enough experience, right?

I just went out and did it – my skateboard background probably responsible for an insatiable desire to stand sideways, and most definitely contributing to the attitude and aptitude of a natural snowboarder. But, as I began showing my friends how to do this cool new sport, I quickly realized not everyone has a background in skating, surfboarding or skiing. Still, there had to be a way to show everyone how to snowboard; so I made a career out of teaching it.

Since starting out telling everyone on crude, unturnable planks to "just point it!" both the sport and how it is taught have come full circle.

Now we look at the biomechanical functions of the body concerning a sideways stance on a piece of fiberglass, wood and steel with a specific sidecut radius moving downhill. Sound complicated? Well, some people still only need to be pointed in the right direction. Others need you to walk them through step-by-step with tons of information. In clinical teaching terms we call it VAK: visual, auditory or kinesthetic learning. You need to either see it, hear it, or feel it, to learn it.

There are simple techniques to help you begin snowboarding, regardless what type of learner you are. There is more than enough information here to start off. In fact, it may be too much. Digest each lesson as needed as you advance through the levels.

Give snowboarding a try. It really is fun, but be patient – the first day is a hard one,

THE NUMBER ONE INJURY IN SNOWBOARDING – A BROKEN WRIST.

and if you've yet to slide sideways it may take a few tries to get the feeling.

But what a feeling!

First day beginner checklist

Safety – The number-one injury in snowboarding is the broken wrist, which can occur when you brace a fall by reaching out with open hands, in front or behind you, to catch yourself. Wrists are very vulnerable to fracture – so keep your hands in balled fists when you bail, to reduce the risks. Supportive wrist guards can also help.

Knee injuries are less common in snowboarding than in skiing, though it is possible to twist an ankle. It's natural to

want to roll out of a fall, but a snowboard will not easily roll with you, and in fact, has inflexible tendencies because of its length, weight and stiffness. I tell my students to fall on to the rear of the snowboard and ride it like a sled when gravity calls.

Helmets remain a personal choice, although two recent high-profile skiing deaths in the States have shown wearing them to be common sense when you're heading downhill at speed.

Balance – Your snowboarding stance should place the hips centered between

HELMETS – STILL A PERSONAL CHOICE.

the feet, not leaning too far forward nor too far back, while standing on the whole foot as much as possible. It is also important not to lean too far in or out of a turn. Keep ankles and knees relaxed and flexed to reduce bending too much at the waist. Overall, go for an athletic body posture with hands raised between hips and chest, palms down, pointing toward the board's nose, and both equal distance away from the body. Think how you'd stand if someone was about to push you over.

Flexibility – Joints and muscles need to be as relaxed as possible. Flexibility helps you do the quick, balanced moves that keep

THE FIRST STEPS – A GOOD STANCE.

you from eating snow. Relaxing your body isn't easy when trying something new, but the easiest way to snowboard is by maintaining a neutral, athletic stance such as a boxer would hold throughout a fight.

Sidecut – All snowboards should have a degree of sidecut. This is the hourglass shape you can see if you look at the base or top of a snowboard from a few feet away. By applying pressure with both feet to the metal edge of the board (toeside or heelside), it will follow the sidecut radius on the side of the board while making the turn. The flatter the base is to the snow when pressure is applied, the more skidded the turn. The higher the angle of the base, the sharper, more carved, the turn will be.

Goofy or regular? – Are you goofy-footed (right foot forward) or regular-footed (left foot forward) when standing on your sled? There is no way to truly tell without experience in skate, surf, or wakeboarding or slalom water-skiing, etc. These sports all have a stance which puts one foot ahead of the other. If you say you've never done any of those, no problem. In most cases the stronger leg is at the rear to support the body and prevent you being too

far back on the board. Try sliding across ice or a slick floor to see which foot naturally flies forward. In general most right-handers are regular-footed and left-handers goofy, though this isn't always the case. If nothing helps, flip a coin to decide. Basically, you will know it when you feel it.

Stance – The angles and width of your bindings are important. Shoulder-width apart is usually a good rule of thumb. Being bow-legged or knock-kneed will have a big effect on your comfort and efficiency. To be balanced and centered, knock-knees should have a narrower stance to help you move from the insides of your feet to flat-footed. Bow-legged people should have a wider stance to help you move off the outsides of your feet. As far as angles go, I suggest experimenting with different positions to find one that feels good and fits your skeletal shape – try forward (towards the nose), flat (towards the center) and negative (rear foot only towards the tail) settings. With greater angles toward the tip of the board, you'll find a greater tendency to make turns straight down the fall-line. With a smaller the angle the more your turns will tend to be across the fall-line. The stance for most all-mountain

freeriding or freestyle riders is 15 degrees in front, zero or slightly angled in back.

"Relax – flexibility keeps you from eating snow!" **Micky Franco**

Attitude – You will fall and may hurt yourself. Don't be embarrassed, or you'll never make it past the first five minutes! Sometimes you have to fail to succeed. After mastering both toeside and heelside turns, you have the know-how to participate in a challenging sport. And then you have no choice but to go to a shop and invest in a mess of expensive gear!

Let's begin

❶ Practise skating around, as if pushing yourself on a skateboard. Start by placing just the lead foot in the binding. This is how you will be travelling in and out of lift lines. One thing to remember for all snowboarding is to keep your shoulders in line with your feet. Otherwise, you create unnecessary rotary movement from twisting the upper body against the lower body. This causes your board to spin when getting off the chairlift – not something you want to have happen. Also, keep the foot that is not attached to the binding pointing the same way as the foot that is. Use the entire length of the inside of your rear foot to push.

NOW THE OBJECT IS TO SLIDE DOWNHILL.

THE GANG ARE GATHERED AND THE LESSON BEGINS.

2 Find a small incline that has a flat or slightly uphill run-out. This is your practice area for getting off the chairlift, and gliding straight to a natural stop. You can practise slight direction changes by lifting up on the toes of the lead foot and applying pressure to the heel edge to make a gradual heel turn. If you lift up on the heel of the lead foot while applying pressure to the toe edge you can make a slight toe turn. Be patient, the board will turn if you let it. Head to the chairlift when comfortable and ready.

3 Getting on the chair looks daunting but is simple. Look over your left or right shoulder towards the middle, depending on which side of the chair you are getting on. As you sit down, lift up both legs so they don't get caught under the chair – most beginner chairs are quite low to the ground. Now sit back and relax!

4 Getting off the chair is possibly the scariest part of learning to ride, yet it does become second nature. Remember in part one when you practised skating around?

This is where that will help. It is important to keep the shoulders in line with the feet, i.e. stand sideways! As you approach the top of the lift, straighten your board so it points forward down the ramp and not sideways like you're standing. Slowly stand up – a centered stance with knees slightly bent and hands out to the side is important to maintain balance. Let the board travel in a straight line to a gentle stop. If you are really nervous, ask the lift attendant to slow the lift down when you get close to the top.

5 This is where the fun starts. Skate to a flat spot at the top of the slope. Put your rear foot in the binding. Feel trapped? You are. Snowboard bindings don't release, nor do you want them to. Stand up, first facing downhill with your board sideways. If this is difficult, grab your toe edge with your trailing hand (towards the tail) and use it to pull you up, and don't forget to move your fingers! Once standing, the object is to slide sideways downhill. The tip and tail of the board should be pointing across the hill, the shoulders and feet pointing up or down-

CLIMBING OFF THE CHAIRLIFT CAN BE TRICKY.

hill, depending on toeside or heelside. Known as a sideslip, this task helps you develop balance and edging skills. The idea is to stay centered while varying pressure on the uphill edge to control the speed of slipping. It is important to not drop the toes too low to the snow or you will catch the downhill edge. Also, your eyes must be looking downhill, not at your feet! Practise controlled stops.

6 When you can sideslip with relative comfort and control, stop, sit down and roll over. It's time to repeat the same for the toeside, with your back to the slope. Once again, don't look down at your feet! Keep your eyes looking slightly uphill. Control the sideslip by standing on the toe edge and easing the pressure to allow the board to slide downhill. Once again it is important to keep the heels from dropping too low and catching the heel edge in the snow!

7 Now for some direction. While sideslipping on the heel edge, apply a very small amount of pressure to the lead foot (towards the nose). Simply push the toes of the lead foot down just a little to add extra weight to the tip. This will allow gravity to pull the tip slightly downhill and across the fall-line, which is the quickest path downhill. If you roll a snowball down the slope the path it takes is the fall-line.

This is called a traverse. It's important to stay centered while doing this. Practise it both forwards and backwards on the toe and heel edge. As you become more comfortable, apply a little more pressure each time to the tip and accelerate down the fall-line. As you accelerate, weight the tail slightly and take the board backwards across the fall-line. This is known as a garland. Finally, practise allowing the tip of the board to seek the fall-line, travel straight downhill for just a moment. Again, steer board backwards across the fall-line.

This drill teaches you the starting and finishing points of the turn.

8 To turn or not to turn? That is the next step! When performing the garland, you pressed the lead foot down and as you accelerated, you shifted your weight back over the tail to take you in the other direction.

Only one thing changes here: as you press down on the lead foot, the board seeks the fall-line. Follow it! When the board has shifted to pointing straight downhill and the base is flat, use both feet to pressure the edge in the direction you want to turn (toeside or heelside), while rotating your shoulders and hips in this new direction across the hill. This will be your first turn. It takes commitment to handle the speed of pointing downhill, but once you pressure the edge, the board will swing around and you can continue pressuring that uphill edge to slow down. Move your body as a complete unit. Don't let your torso get ahead of your feet or vice versa.

EVERYONE – EXPERTS AND BEGINNERS – TAKES A TUMBLE AT ONE STAGE.

Let's review for a minute

Heelside sideslip – Stand on heel edge, press both toes down slightly and evenly, taking pressure off heels, allowing the board to slide gradually downhill. Pressure heels and lift up on toes to control speed. Hands out at your sides, shoulders in line with feet for balance.

Toeside sideslip – Stand on toe edge, press both heels down slightly and evenly, taking pressure off toes, allowing board to slide gradually downhill. Pressure toes and lift up on heels to control speed. Hands out at sides, shoulders in line with feet for balance.

Heelside traverse – From heelside sideslip, apply slight pressure to lead foot by pushing down the toes of the lead foot while maintaining a centered stance. Pull up on lead foot to even pressure to heel edge and sideslip again or to stop.

Toeside traverse – From toeside sideslip, apply slight pressure to lead foot by pushing down the heel of the lead foot while maintaining a centered stance. Pull up on lead heel to even pressure to toe edge and sideslip again or to stop.

Heelside garland – Push down on toes of lead foot, turn hips and shoulders sideways until board seeks the fall-line. After sufficient travel, lift up on lead toes and rotate hips, shoulders and head back towards the tail to travel backwards on toe edge across the fall-line.

Toeside garland – Push down on heels of lead foot and turn hips and shoulders sideways until board seeks the fall-line. After sufficient travel, lift up on lead heel and rotate hips, shoulders and head back towards the tail to travel backwards on heel edge across the fall-line.

Heelside turn – Start with toeside sideslip. Next, do first phase of toeside garland. When board points downhill and base is flat, gradually pressure heel edge with both feet, following through with whole body, rotating shoulders and hips through the turn, finishing in same position as heelside sideslip. Movement should be smooth and gradual, body in one line, never twisted.

Toeside turn – Start with heelside sideslip, then the first phase of heelside garland. When board points downhill and base is flat, gradually pressure toe edge with both feet, following through with whole body, rotating shoulders and hips through the turn, finishing in same position as toeside sideslip. Movement should be smooth and gradual, body in one line, never twisted.

"Don't get too confident too soon!"
Micky Franco

You've completed your first lesson. How does it feel? Once you've linked your first turns together it's important to practise and develop a strong sense of balance before moving on to other skills or harder terrain. Don't get too confident too soon – this is the stage where most beginner/intermediates have their hardest falls. Remember, you're still learning. Practise linking turns to ensure you have a good grasp of the basics to build on.

Tips to develop your turning skills

Adding a few movements to your first linked, skidded turns will take you to the next level of snowboarding. Move your center of mass (the point on the body of the greatest concentration of weight) across the board as you finish your turn. This will help you develop turn shape by engaging the edge and utilizing the sidecut of the board. Dynamic turn shape will also help control speed. To make heelside turns more dynamic, roll the lead knee toward the tip of the board and allow your hips to move downhill across the board at the initiation of the turn. For toeside turns, move the knee of the lead foot over the toes of the lead foot towards the tip and through the turn.

The better you can do this the closer you will be to carving turns, where the tail of the board follows in the exact line of the tip. It may take some time to develop. There is a great deal of balance needed to put the board up on edge.

In skidded and dynamic skidded turns, the board is allowed to slide around the turn with the edge not very angled against the snow. To increase the edge's angle to the snow, a dynamic body movement across the board and downhill is needed. The ankles need to be

ONCE YOU HAVE MASTERED THE BASICS YOU CAN DEVELOP THOSE SKILLS!

flexed initially, and then locked once a high enough edge angle is met. Keep ankles locked until you've run the edge. Then, a lateral, dynamic, downhill movement of the body is needed for the next turn. To feel a carve, allow the shape of the board to dictate the size and shape of the turn.

As you begin to explore more and more of the mountain, one thing will either help or hinder you: patience. Snowboards allow people to go places sooner, and with less ability. Don't let that quick learning curve convince you that you're ready for expert runs before you have conquered the advanced ones. Be patient with your learning to avoid bad habits and prevent injury.

Terrain selection will help you avoid dangerous situations. Weather is the primary factor in choosing terrain, something as simple as, which way did the wind blow? Observations about your surroundings will help you find good snow and keep you away from areas where the snow is rotten, sun-cupped or has been scoured by the wind.

At the Jackson Hole Mountain Resort where I work, most major weather fronts come from the west. Large, unprotected west-facing slopes are subject to the high winds of the storm. This is referred to as the windward side. The eastern side of the mountain, in this case, is the leeward side. It receives wind-transported snow.

Sun exposure will help determine if the snow gets soft or hard. South-facing aspects of the mountain get a great deal of sun and have a tendency to be icy in the morning, slushy in the afternoon. On north-facing aspects, very little sun hits, which has a tendency to keep the snow cold and more consistent.

There is a lot to learn. The more time you spend around mountains the more you can pick up, all of which will make you a better, more knowledgeable snowboarder.

Here are some tips on dealing with what you might encounter:

Crud, slop, chowder, mush – or whatever you call snow that's not powder and not groomed – presents its own demands. The most important riding skill to use is flexibility. The ability to keep the muscles relaxed and constantly in motion is crucial. Once your muscles become static or still, you can get bounced off the mountain! At times, crud may drag the tip of your board under the snow. Vertical motion, or raising the body to help unweight the board, may be of some assistance here. It's also important to keep the eyes two or three turns ahead to anticipate any problems.

Steeps are my specialty! The most important thing to remember about steeps is to stay on the ground. Hop turns are only for fun in good snow. When you hop a turn you are leaving the ground, and when you leave the ground you lose control. That's not something you want to happen when a fall could mean serious injury.

"Attitude – you will have fun!"
Mickey Franco

The ideal turn is the tip roll, a combination of three things: 1) Retract the rear leg, lifting the tail of the board slightly off the snow while the tip stays down. 2) Move the body across the board toward the fall-line. 3) Rotate the hips and shoulders into the next turn.

What's happening is you are lifting the tail and moving the body across the fall-line. As the tail crosses the fall-line, set the edge. It is crucial that you stay as centered as possible. Too much weight towards the tip may make you to go 'over the bars', pitching over the nose. It is also important to look towards the finish of your turn, which will help keep your body in alignment. You can keep the fall-line in focus by always keeping it in your peripheral vision. Take a

look at the fall-line as you anticipate your next turn. Don't get sucked in to staring straight downhill all the time. This can cause you to move your body straight downhill all the time, causing loss of turn shape and poor speed control.

Moguls or 'bumps' teach you two important things: 1) To look ahead. This helps create a proactive or offensive approach to your riding. You will find that riding defensively or reactively in uneven terrain will soon have you completely worn out and out of control. The time it takes to react to the terrain, tell your brain what to do and actually do it is too much. By the time your muscles respond you'll already be into the next turn. 2) To absorb. It is essential to remain relaxed and flexible to handle uneven terrain. By predicting what the bump will do to your board, you can retract the legs before you hit the bump with full impact and extend them just as you begin to ride over the top.

"You'll soon feel that you're on your way to freestyle Nirvana!"
Mickey Franco

Try spinning without the board at first. Stand with your feet a little wider than shoulder width. Jump up and try to rotate 360 degrees by spinning your feet only. How far did you get? Now try to rotate using your head, hands, and shoulders. Try the same maneuver by rotating just your hips, and you'll see they're the best source to use in a spin. It is very important however, to look in the direction of your rotation. You must turn your head at the beginning. If your body spins and your head doesn't, it will stop the rotation just short of where you want to be. Put these together with the jump tips and soon you'll see and feel that you're on your way to freestyle Nirvana.

Don't forget riding fakie, and the trick to that is in the binding angles. If you have a low or negative (towards the tail) angle on your rear binding, the riding technique is the same as riding forward. If your rear foot is cocked towards the nose you will have to compensate. Remaining centered is the most fundamental aspect of doing a fakie or switch-stance. The difficult part is the fact that you just spent a great deal of time and effort to train your brain and muscles to perform a certain task. Now you're asking them to do all of them in reverse.

Finally, though it's covered in another chapter, here are thoughts on the mechanics of jumping, spinning and riding fakie (backwards), since it's easily the most popular part of learning to ride!

When learning to jump you must spot your landings! You never know who or what is lying under the jump. Avoid what could be a dangerous mistake. The first step is learning to take off and land on a flat base. Standing on the whole of the foot is the best balance point. The knees must remain flexed. Balance on take-off is critical. It will determine whether you land on your feet or your head. As you approach a jump keep your body aligned, which will help you travel straight and forward off the hit. Hands must be out and ready to make adjustments. Start off by riding over smaller jumps with no leg retraction or vertical motion. As you get comfortable, add a little rising just before take-off, followed by quick retraction of the legs, held until you land. Soon you'll be flying and landing with ease.

Landing jumps has a lot to do with what and where you are jumping. Flat landings are not so good for the back and knees, and can lead to early retirement. Stick with jumps that have a nice, steep landing and plenty of run-out room to stop – remember the chairlift? As you are about to land, don't focus too much on the landing zone. Just know where it is so you are prepared for what's to come. As you come down, extend the legs out to meet the landing. As you touch down, absorb impact by retracting the legs. You will accelerate as soon as you touch down, so it helps to know where you're going to slow down and stop.

Learning to ride fakie takes a little more patience, because it's not the way you are comfortable. You need to learn to trust your instinct that you'll land, rather than twist and look which will cause the landing to go wrong anyway. But in the long run it isn't just helpful with freestyle riding. It is a skill that will get out of emergency situations where you might be thrown backwards and have to ride that way to recover your balance.

Tricks of the trade

By Eric Wright

So you can ride. Now bust a few stylish new moves

or nearly all snowboarding enthusiasts, performing some kind of trick is a highlight of the experience.

Okay, so doing stunts is not a requirement, nor does your allowable fun hinge on your ability to perform them. There are snowboarders who couldn't care less about tricks – making fresh powder turns or running laps down the slopes provides the satisfaction they are looking for.

But if you have ever opened a snowboarding magazine, or viewed a snowboarding movie, you will know the attraction of tricks for hardcore fans. They strive to emulate their idols' feats in the hope of landing a page of their own in a mag, or a shot in someone's movie – of completing a perfect performance with suave, smooth style – in their heads, at least, if nowhere else. And from every painful fall they get up humbly to continue down the path towards becoming a master or mistress of tricks.

One reason they call snowboarding a 'lifestyle' sport is it takes a lifetime of effort

TRICKS ARE THE HIGHLIGHT OF THE BOARDER'S TRADE.

to learn all one is capable of doing. Some of the expert rotating moves like 540s, 900s, and rodeo flips take years to accomplish. With boundless imagination and ingenuity, the progression never has to stop, meaning that every rider can imprint their personal style on to, say, an aerial. Originality is the key; it's what keeps snowboarding advancing every day there's snow in the mountains. There's no right or wrong way to ride – it's all in your outlook.

Don't be intimidated by the time factor. Sure, it takes years to become a 'master', but that doesn't mean your first week, or even first day, can't be spent having fun doing tricks. This chapter should help you figure out the learning process.

Evolution

Every snowboard trick you perform directly or indirectly stems from skateboarding – the knowledge has been passed down like an old pair of jeans to a younger sibling. Having your feet strapped in does place a limit on some of the possibilities skateboarding offers, but nonetheless you will find most maneuvers easier and less painful.

Surfing has also had a profound influence on snowboarding. Not so much in the way of tricks, more in style – dropping in on a sloped transition and the Spiccoli Factor. "It's all about looking at a wave and saying, hey bud, let's party!", as the surf guru said.

It's important to recognize the impact both of these sports have had on snowboarding. Edging a snowboard to turn takes its skill from these sports rather than from skiing. Some skiers take pleasure in pointing out that skis are transportation devices and that a snowboard is a toy, but they can have it. A toy – that's right – all fun, baby!

Also important to remember is the amount of different terrain one can ride on a snowboard. One trick will vary depending on where you execute it. You can perform moves in halfpipes, snowboard parks, off

cliffs, over rollers, on handrails – a veritable plethora of media to exploit in your personal snowboarding expression.

The idea of practising may remind you of a tedious, rote task that more resembles work than fun. But that doesn't apply to snowboarding. Acquiring these skills is about enjoying yourself in a beautiful, awe-inspiring setting – the outdoors in winter.

Start slow and follow each proper step. You have to learn a 180 and have it dialed before you can expect to spin a switch 540. But don't focus so much on advancing your skills that you lose sight of the true prize, that of playing the game.

Tricky terminology

Frontside – This describes the direction you are going in when you do a trick. It originates from surfing, referring to the direction you are going in up a wave when you turn to face it with your chest. If you are a regular-foot snowboarder (left foot forward) and you're looking down the pipe, the right wall would be your frontside. Vice versa for goofy-footers (right foot forward).

Backside – This also comes from surfing, and is the opposite of frontside. As you come up the halfpipe wall with your back to the lip, you're going backside.

Fakie (switch-stance) – Going fakie is going backwards. This term comes from skateboarding and applies to the philosophy of doing tricks while riding your board the opposite way of your normal stance (goofy- or regular-foot). Riding 'switch' adds a new dimension of difficulty, making every trick twice as hard as you are riding in the opposite direction of what feels comfortable.

One of the first 'tricks' you can practise to increase board mastery (and a sure way to jack up the difficulty on any trick you can do) is the art of riding backwards/ fakie/switch-stance.

Shall we begin?

To get you started these are three beginner moves that work well together. Practise them. Get them dialed. A great snowboarder is only as good as his or her fundamentals.

a Ride at a comfortable speed, standing upright with your arms by your side.

b Bend your knees and start to crouch.

c Here's the trick – as you start your ollie place all the weight on your back foot and lift the nose of your board. This is the moment you propel yourself upward.

The ollie

The most fundamental trick in snowboarding, the ollie must be learned before any progression can begin. The trick was invented in the late 70s by skateboarder Allen Gelfand. It is a basic no-handed aerial where you use only a combination of foot movements and momentum to propel yourself upward while controlling the board. Having your feet strapped to a snowboard makes this easier, but it still takes practice to get the timing down.

d The nose comes up first, then you lift your back leg and level out. The more you compact your body, putting your knees into your chest, the more lift you'll get.

e

Frontside air (in the pipe)

First, you need to be able to do a frontside turn in the pipe all the way to the top. Then do it carrying enough speed to go about two feet past that point. Learn at a comfortable pace, so you don't fly out of control and end up eight feet out of the pipe only to land on your neck somewhere down in the flat bottom. Imagine the wall of the pipe is actually twenty feet taller and you just want to make a turn as high as you can.

d Let your tail ride off the lip as you bring your knees to your chest.

c Ride off the lip. Don't jump. Just continue riding upward.

b Ride up the wall, absorbing the transition and slowly raising your arms for upward momentum.

a Ride across the flat bottom with your arms hanging at your sides and your knees bent.

e As you reach your high point, reach down and grab between your feet.

f As you start to release the grab, spot where you will land and point your shoulders there. Land as high on the wall as possible and absorb the tranny down and into the flats where you will again be riding with your arms hanging at your side.

Backside air (in the pipe)

d

Practise the technique of doing this without a grab and when you feel confident, raise your feet to the bac[k] of your neck, reach down, and grab.

e

Landing backside is much easier than frontside because you can see exactly where you're going. **Hint:** Don't pull off the transition too hard, as it is easy to land out in the flats on backside airs.

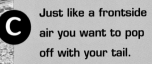

c Just like a frontside air you want to pop off with your tail.

b Flatten out, absorb the tranny going up, and start to raise your arms for upward momentum.

a Ride across the flats on your heel edge with your arms hanging.

For some reason, backside airs present a problem for most snowboarders. Maybe it's because your back is to the lip, making it hard to see what's going on, so you have to rely more on feel and timing. This takes a lot of practice.

Someone once told me that a good backside air starts in the flat bottom. On your approach to the wall you must be firmly on edge, which requires proper forward lean on your highback bindings. Then you must transfer to riding a flat base at the same time you are absorbing the tranny and raising your arms.

Frontside 180

Spinning to win

As you get comfortable doing straight airs and landing, the next step is to add in spin. The sport has evolved to the 1080-degree stage of rotations – three complete 360s – but we will stick to basics and you can decide for yourself when to embark on that quest. If you do, spin and keep on going.

e

Turning your shoulders is the key to this trick. Rotate your upper body and let the legs follow so that you land facing the direction you're going.

f

Land and absorb the shock.

a First of all, survey the jump, figure out the landing, and gauge the speed necessary to make it from point a to point b.

b When you know you can safely make it to the landing zone without coming up short or overshooting it and breaking your back, hike up and drop in.

d It is important to just ride off the lip and allow the momentum to propel you. As you reach the peak of your air, turn your shoulders frontside and start to bring your knees up.

c Ride to the jump with your arms down and relaxed.

Fakie to forward

In skateboarding this trick is called a half-Cab because it's half a Caballerial, a trick named after its inventor, skateboarder Steve Caballero. It means to ride up backwards and rotate around to forward. But, since Steve came out publicly and stated that on a snowboard you're inferior, the trick has adopted the technical name of fakie to forward. Who's gonna argue with an original member of the Bones Brigade?

e This should be easier to land than the 180 because you're coming back to your normal direction. It will be harder to take off though, that's why it's important to gather yourself in the air before you start spinning or sticking your tongue out.
Hint: The more you pull your knees up the more time you give yourself to rotate.

d The key to this trick is pulling your knees up as much as you can while spreading your arms (it can't hurt to poke your tongue out like Michael Jordan either).

a Learn to ride your snowboard backwards (or fakie, or switch-stance).

b Carry the same amount of speed you would for a frontside 180.

c Ride off the lip and gather yourself in the air. Just like a 180, you want to turn your shoulders the direction you are going.

Backside 360

This trick is easier than it looks, but requires timing to make it look good. You want to rotate as one unit and not the herky-jerky, throw-your-body, muscle-it-around, I'm-from-Moosejaw, wherever, backside "Yeah, guy!"

a Initiate this spin from your toes and carry it through with your shoulders.

b Ride toward the jump with a flat base or on your heel edge and as you approach the take off, load all your weight onto your toes.

c Simultaneously rotate your head and shoulders backside and begin your spin.

d The best way to get that sucker around is to keep looking where you want to go. If you're facing that way, your body will catch up.

e Think about compacting your body as much as possible, the more lanky and dangling your body is, the less likely it is to spin.

f As you come around spot the landing and land square on both feet.

g Ride away back to Moosejaw and treat yourself to a bear claw!

Rodeo Flip

A real hardcore trick, this is one to aspire to, that we've included here to show you some potential. there's no instructions, becuase it is just too dangerous until you're getting good. Don't try this at home.

Want to be a pro?

Exposing the illusion of sponsorship grandeur.

By Matthew Linnell

It's sleight of hand, magic, an illusion. Using a wand, the magician encourages you to watch carefully. He pulls the cover shot out of his hat – 50 feet of sheer vertical drop – a snowboarder mysteriously suspended in time. The board is hanging above the untouched powder landing, falling below blue sky. During any video frame, on any given page it's the same routine, but never the same cliff. Not the identical amount of rotations; never the same fragmented second. So sit and watch the rest of the magician's act knowing he will link the rings, saw the woman in half, make the Bengal tiger vanish, and turn flowers into fire.

Second-hand snowboarding is a grand illusion – not because what you are shown isn't real, but because the essence is what is not shown – the tracks just out of frame, riders lined up on the cliff top, the hours of travelling, waiting for blue skies. The other shots from that same hit that had to be weeded through before finding this one.

For some, bearing witness to the act isn't enough. They ask to be in on the secret, to see the two-way mirrors, expose the trap door and know how the woman is halved and made whole again. They ask, "How do I get sponsored, how do I become a pro?" But to answer, the magician's code must be discarded, the miraculous has to be revealed and the spell is inevitably broken. Be warned – once you're shown the secret glass panel all you may see is your own reflection.

To partake of the knowledge, one must step out of the theater and into the waiting green room. Once inside, you can hear from different levels of performers: the dinner-table conjurer turning tricks for friends, the corner magician hustling the shell game or three-card monte, barely making rent, the talented few who make it to the big stage as professional illusionists.

Then there is the matter of how to become a part of it; what different qualities are needed to make a valued performer, the work expected, the backstage set-up and the unseen tasks, all as much a part of the performance as were volcanic eruptions and epic snowstorms in the creation of the mountains and snowfields we ride. The list goes on and on. The palms, holds, flips, switches, changeovers and other sleights-of-hand revealed. If you want to be a pro, watch carefully: there's nothing up my sleeves, but don't take your eye off the wand for a moment.

freestyle, freeriding and extreme riding sponsorships

These deals are all about *exposure*. You can drop the biggest cliffs and rule the newest tricks, but if your performance doesn't make it on film, you will have a hard time finding support.

The different levels of sponsorship are not cut and dried. This is the basic structure, although you can enter the game at any level and rise at any speed.

Pro-form/shop sponsored

This is the kid who comes into the snowboard shop all the time, buys the equipment and practises his tricks. He or she shows promise, but more than anything, has real enthusiasm.

The pro-form itself (more often called a 'bro-form') is an order sheet offered to everyone from snowboard instructors to shop employees and offers a just-below-wholesale price for equipment. It is often the first step for pros on their way.

This can be combined with a shop sponsorship, where the rider is expected to promote the shop. Many pro riders have a real loyalty to their home shop and shops sponsor everyone from amateurs to world champions.

Amateur/regional sponsored

This is the dinner-table conjurer eager to display skills at any time. Regional amateur snowboarders usually get this type of sponsorship through a sales rep in their region.

At best they might receive one board, a pair of boots and clothing for free. They are expected to ride their local area and compete. They get no financial support or travel money since they rarely receive magazine or video coverage. They're encouraged to give the rep feedback on any equipment problems and suggest design ideas.

Pro-am

These riders resemble the newly-initiated street magician performing tricks and sleights for an unexpected audience – an occasional photographer or interested film-maker looking for new talent. Their success depends on how naturally they take to new situations and how well they have developed their own personal style.

This grey area between amateur and pro is common among sponsored riders and usually means they receive a couple of boards, financial help towards a season pass and an opportunity to make incentives if they get photos or video coverage. These riders receive no salary and rarely any travel money. They may or may not compete and probably have other income to pay daily expenses. At this point it's not usual to get media coverage.

IF YOU ARE LUCKY YOU CAN BE PAID TO HAVE FUN.

FOR SOME THIS IS WORK.

Rider Jim Smith spent the early days of his snowboarding career in this zone: "After I left high school," he says, "I moved to Breckenridge and worked at a Mexican restaurant cooking and washing dishes. For a few years I did that and really scraped to get by. I got to ride a lot and made a lot of friends. For all those years I was working I really wasn't making that much at all. I was getting contracts, I was signing contracts, but the contracts were generally for one board and I would, like, break the board and usually have to get more."

Pro

By this point these hustling corner musicians are mastering skills and style but must work every angle and opportunity – the shell game or three-card monte – in order to get paid. Once a rider reaches this level they usually get equipment as they need it and have fairly extensive lists of sponsors. On average they're making a small salary, but only just scraping by. Most riders will be allocated a travel budget for photo shoots or contests. They could be getting more consistent coverage in magazines and videos or placing in contests for pro purses.

Jim Smith, now considered a pro, explains his current situation: "I get a lot of product and they pay my rent and stuff, but I don't live large by any means. I don't own anything other than a lot of snowboards and a lot of snowboard clothing, like I don't own car or a TV and I don't have a permanent place to live. I have a skateboard, a Game Gear and my snowboards. I don't really have any material items, but it is totally worth it for me."

Established pro

These are the stage illusionists, travelling several times a year to different locations to perform their act. They are recognised by name, have a distinct style and play a role in designing their equipment. The established pro pays his or her bills and then some with their salary, has a season pass provided, plus travel expenses and total product flow. He or she usually gets consistent coverage in films, videos, magazines and may be a top finisher in pro tour and World Cup contests. He or she spends a considerable part of the year travelling.

Former professional snowboarder Tucker Fransen describes his past lifestyle: "I had been getting paid for probably seven years, ever since I was in high school but it's never like I've been a millionaire glam-rocker guy. I've just been kind of struggling along. In the summertime I worked with my dad doing refrigeration, and that's how I'd make extra money. And during the winter I rode a lot." Fransen now has a job with a snowboard manufacturer.

"Most of these guys are out there working. They wouldn't be getting the coverage if they weren't working."
Terry Kidwell

VIDEO COVERAGE PAYS WELL TOO!

Super pro

These are the David Copperfields of the snowboarding world, making up the top 15 to 20 riders on the planet. They make a comfortable living and are able to save considerably if so inclined. Most riders at this level have a signature model board, dominate videos and magazines and spend the entire year travelling and snowboarding. They have plenty of opportunities for royalties and endorsement outside traditional sponsorship.

"When I won, it was only a handful of people who could really ride the pipe. And now it's 50 or 60 guys who are really, really hot in the pipe with a couple of big standouts like Terje (Haakonsen). When I watch Terje ride, it's like a whole other world. He's just a step above everybody."
Terry Kidwell

Veteran consummate professional Shaun Palmer relates: "I've been doing it for 10 (now 12) years. I was flying all over the place when I was 15, dropping out of school because of it – I made a career out of it, you know. I could have chosen to go to school – I chose snowboarding. With everything going on with me at the time, it was the right thing to do. I didn't see getting too much out of sitting in an algebra class. I see more, learn more out of being on a big peak with powder everywhere. I've got a good career going for me."

racing sponsorships

Alpine racers are the Vaudeville jugglers of the stage, the ones who survive on an exhibition of pure talent alone. Their deals are based solely on contest results.

THE ONLY SNOWBOARDERS WHO HAVE A LUXURY LIFESTYLE ARE THE SUPER-PROS.

"When you're home –
you want to get away.
But as you get away,
it's like home is
where everything's at.
Home-cooked meal,
bed you can sleep in.
You really appreciate
it when you're gone."
Pro Joe Curtes

HOME LIFE CAN BE HARD – YOU ARE ALWAYS ON THE MOVE

Amateur Alpine racer

These are the up-and-coming jugglers, the talented few who show enough discipline and raw talent to attain the high level of skill needed for the professional realm. Riders will have very similar contracts to the amateur freerider or freestyle rider: one or two boards, clothes, boots and maybe some help with entry fees.

WEARING A SHOP'S EQUIPMENT IS A GOOD START.

With the United States Skiing Association's (USSA) creation of a US snowboarding team there are big opportunities for the very top amateur competitors in America. The USSA provides and pays all travel, training, entry fees and living expenses for members of their team.

The United States Amateur Snowboarding Association (USASA) continues to provide amateur competition and controls the sport's loyalty and best athletes, but remains grassroots without funds to sponsor individuals.

Pro Alpine racer

Street-performing analogies follow here, but these performers spend more money on equipment and training than they collect in their hat at the end of each show. Most professional Alpine racers struggle to break even. They are very lucky if training, travel and entry fees are paid for. Most racers are spending more on coaching than they earn. They must participate in an extreme training regimen to stay competitive and Alpine racing is such a small part

of the snowboard market that riders receive no film or video coverage and limited competition television exposure.

Underdog pro Antonio Davilla explains the reality: "I am pretty much footing the bill completely. I've spent seven to eight thousand dollars in training. On top of that there are housing, travel and entry fees. A friend of mine, Jasey Jay Anderson, competes really well and is placed top three in every pro event he goes to. He is in just as much financial worry as I am right now and he really hammered some results out." Both are still racing.

Top pro Alpine racer

The racing world does support a tiny number of the best riders, those who compare to the world's greatest juggler Anthony Gatos or to big-time Vegas acts who can keep an astonishing amount of objects in the air. This group comprises the top eight to 10 racers on the planet. Only here are racers paid all-expenses, make good salaries and receive multiple endorsements – and this is mostly in Europe where racing

SPONSORSHIP COMES WHEN YOU DESERVE IT!

"Travelling all around the world sounds glamorous, but it is tough work staying up long hours, with mixed-up sleep schedules, snowboarding all the time, being on stage, having to perform in front of a group of people in Japan who are expecting you to do something incredible when you're tired. It is a lot tougher than people think."
Industry mogul Tim Pogue

gets media play. Even these top pros receive little snowboard video or magazine coverage, where most of the market deals its hand. Income is completely dependent on race results and contest winnings, which can be good money.

the spotlight

Who controls it, how to get in it

You've been handed the program, you know what comes when, but the order of accomplishment alone offers little insight into the inner workings of sponsorship. Let's take a reality check.

Paul Ferrel, Mervin Manufacturing team manager, explains his take: "Sponsorship will come to riders who deserve it. If they are really interested in winning support, the best way to start is participate in local snowboarding contests. If they hook up with a local shop, their chances of being sponsored are much higher." Ferrel also mentions that sponsorship is no automatic award for riders who reach a certain level. Sponsorship is given to those who stand out as very special among their talented peers.

Tim Pogue, former vice-president of Ride Snowboards, now a retail business-man, explains the difference between the good and the gifted: "I think there is a whole attitude ... because they can do a backside 360 they think they deserve something. I'm 32 years old and I can do a backside 360."

Beyond the obvious requirement of real ability and polished skills, different people offer varied advice about how to get noticed. Industry marketing veteran Brad Steward, who claims to have signed over 300 riders between Sims, Morrow and Bonfire, the clothing brand he started, explains his philosophy: "There are a lot of things you can do, and one of them is to break the rules of sponsorship. What I mean is to forget this whole idea of a resumé, a video ... I urge kids to find a unique angle. For advertising at Bonfire we always seek out that kid who has done something a little odd."

Initial sponsorship has to do with being noticed in your region as an exceptional rider and an individual, usually by a local shop or company rep. But what happens after your first free board? What qualities are valuable to a company?

Paul Ferrel describes his company characteristics: "We are looking for good people who get along and are social and polite, because they are representing our company. Later on, after the rider progresses through levels of sponsorship, their input on the product becomes valuable because it is pretty rare to find someone who understands and knows board design, materials and stuff like that."

When will the spotlight dim?

Only a talented few learn to levitate or walk through walls and go on to perform their tricks on the stages of the world. How long can one captivate the crowd? Trevor Graves, an ace photographer and the creative director of Morrow Snowboards, puts it this way: "Let's say you get discovered at Mount Hood (Oregon). If everything goes well, you have a sponsor with the money to put you on the road and get you where you can be filmed and shot for articles. You'll probably be on the road for a solid three years after that initial discovery. While injuries shorten that life expectancy quite a bit, legendary status lengthens it. People like Craig Kelly, Terje Haakonsen, Jamie Lynn and a few others are people who have that super-pro status. They will be able to stay on top of it."

Behind the scenes

Before you sabotage that pizza delivery truck, shine your boss and head for Mount Hood, realize you must go backstage to see what's really involved. Tucker Fransen speaks about the reality behind the illusion that a pro just rides powder year-round: "It's not like you're out there riding all day, all the time. In between you gotta work with shops and help out the company a little bit. It's not like I totally just get to go out and snowboard and get paid to do that. There is a lot more involved than that."

This aspect of the work behind being a professional snowboarder isn't apparent to

IT CAN BE HARD WORK BEING A PRO – LONG HOURS WAITING FOR THE RIGHT SHOT.

most aspiring riders. Former Burton team manager Eric Kotch describes the routine: "It's going out and visiting shops and doing promos and sitting in the shop for hours and answering questions. If you're a competitor, it's having to sit outside in cold, shitty weather to do a contest all day. Going out and shooting and filming – that's work too, even though it's fun, it's still work. All aspects of what pros do is work, it's just that some of it's fun and some sucks."

Brad Steward elaborates: "You've got to meet with this photographer who has to shoot these kinds of images. You've got to make sure he gets that photo to us on this date ... it's being in the right videos, being in the magazines, having the awareness that extends past going out and riding powder all the time. And it's also having an awareness of when it is time to go and just ride powder. It's having a responsibility and awareness that even though you work for a company and work with a company as a rider, to a certain extent you work for yourself, you are your own franchise."

How big is the Big Time?

Being a pro is more self-employment or self-promotion than is apparent. It's like the accomplished street hustler who has to decide when to move to the stage and when to enjoy working his tricks in the alley. It isn't just riding with your buddies while sponsors land your career, but it still sounds attractive. Doing demos, contests, autograph sessions, travel, design work and photo shoots sounds a lot better than throwing dough or washing up at Krustie's Kitchen, and you'd be making a lot more money, right? Well, maybe.

"Maybe it's getting ruined for everyone."
Tim Swart

"Before, there weren't too many people making a living, and it seems like a lot more people can now. But maybe it's getting ruined for everyone because it's all spreading out so thin and everyone is getting less," speculates former Airwalk, now Spy Eyewear team manager Tim Swart.

Brad Steward explains the unbalanced distribution of wealth among pro snowboarders: "I think there are 20 riders in America who are making a lot of money

"From 1984 to about 1990 it was pretty much all contest. Back then if you didn't do contests it was hard to get sponsored. Now it's totally different. You can make a living off the sport just by going out and filming and shooting photos, which is really cool. Contests are fun and everything but it really isn't snowboarding."
'Father of freestyle' Terry Kidwell

THIS IS THE BEST; YOU GET TO SNOWBOARD WHEN YOU WORK.

and that's it. Everyone else is still at a struggling level. I don't think beyond that you can have people who are making the kind of income where they can buy a new car and house, (the things) that slowly become important to them."

Perhaps the question you must answer for yourself is how much you want. Tim Swart puts it this way: "What do you consider 'making it'? Is it making a lot of money, or is it getting a free pass and not having to wash any more dishes? That's what matters the most for some people, and other people it matters if they are able to buy a house or something. It's relative."

The future

What will the life of a pro be like in a year? In five years? In a decade? In the 1940s, at the height of Vaudeville, magicians and jugglers were more plentiful than stand-up comedians are today, but when television overtook the stage the performers had to change too. In a sport that deals in quantum leaps, one must always have his or her eye on the future.

"It used to be three, four years ago a rider was chosen on their riding ability and their contest results," says Eric Kotch. "Now selection is still based on riding ability, but also on names and images, on straight-up marketability – sometimes over riding. In four or five years it's going to come down to true professionals, to the people who can represent the company in the best way and can really ride."

Brad Steward sees a change coming in the importance of the pro and their signature snowboard model: "There are two gaps to be settled, and one is that economically, it's going to be harder for companies to pay those higher salaries. I think that as snowboarding spreads out, people are going to care less in general about the signature model aspect. It will always be a huge part

"It's great being sponsored, but there's a lot of bad things too. When they want to take you to a shop and do a shop demo – it's kind of stupid some-times. Some kids get stoked on you 'cause you're signing an autograph for them. I don't really understand that, I mean, you're just signing your name for them."
**Super pro
Shaun Palmer**

of the market, maybe the biggest, but (shops are) still going to be able to sell a $379 all-around snowboard without a spe-cial brand name on it."

Ironically, ski companies are now also testing the market for signature skis which feature signed endorsements from the world's best skiers.

Tim Swart speculates changes are already taking place: "I don't think that the industry can sustain any more pros, there are too many in the spotlight right now. Maybe it's going back to a few. I don't think that companies can be promoting riders only. They're going to be involved in product feedback and working for their money, not just being a name promoted in ads, an image. Riders must be prepared to work harder too, promoting companies more than just hanging out and having the com-panies fly them all over for photos."

The biggest trick
Now you've got the future, the past, the pros and cons and you're desperate to buy a Filofax, start lurking at trade shows and bugging your local shop 'til they give you something. But you haven't answered the most important question of all: Why?

Jim Smith puts it this way: "It would depend on the kid's attitude. If he was like, 'Yeah, I want to get sponsored, I want to get free stuff,' this and that, I would tell him to not do it, to go to college. If the kid was like, 'Damn dude, I love snowboarding so much and I just want to ride powder,' and wasn't focussed on the whole sponsorship thing, I would be like, 'Let me hook you up with someone.'" Jim is talking about values. What is the emphasis? A love for riding, or for free equipment, exposure and status?

Eric Kotch's comments echo the sentiment: "Go out and just ride. Do what you love to do. Don't snowboard because you want to get sponsored, snowboard because that's what you love to do. If you really love to do it and you're good at snow-boarding, someone's going to notice it and they're going to pay you for doing what you love to do – that's what it's all about."

But even if you've got the love, consider some of the consequences before you step on the first rung of the pro ladder. Paul Ferrel makes a cautionary point: "One thing I tell people when they do become a sponsored rider is that they are giving up snowboarding as their original outlet, where they would go snowboarding for themselves."

Brad Steward offers these final thoughts: "One of the things we ask our rid-ers to do is to have a reason for being on that team that goes way beyond being in the magazines. No offense to the maga-zines, but have a reason that you're into it above that, and have a reason that you're into it above the economic side of it. The best thing is to come into the sponsor thing protecting one side of your life, and that is your ability to have fun rid-ing. When that's gone, no amount of money in the world will make it come back."

The real trick is to never forget why you became a performer in the first place – for the magic. Not the act, but the mysterious rush of adrenaline and fluidity that anyone can experience with four feet of wood on their feet sliding down a snow-covered hill.

Antonio Davilla expresses it best: "Regardless of whether I have a sponsor or not, I am still having fun and it is still my favorite thing to do. That's the bottom line, you know?"

The Tao of physics, the point
of diminishing returns and
the man who didn't want
a million dollars

Craig Kelly

By Jeff Galbraith

The winningest, most stylish rider in the sport revealed.

"As manifested in today's environment, it is extremely hazardous to compete with five million out-of-control human beings endlessly copulating and bowing to the gods of growth and planned waste, rewarded with IOU paper promises to their non-existent Promised Land. Getaway is the name of the game and I've been burning up the road ever since." **Legendary surfer Mickey Dora**

before he ever won a thing, we knew. In the dark recesses of the old Mt Baker lodge a friend pointed over rows of soaking wet ski school punks and said, "That's him. That's Craig Kelly and he's going to win it all." Which sounds far more dramatic now, considering that at the time, 1986, there wasn't a whole lot to win. It's also a notion with which, throughout the years, Craig has never been entirely comfortable.

Of course he went on to win four world championships, a car or two, money, notoriety and the unfailing respect of nearly every rider on the planet. Ironically, he became so good, so consistent, such a model of hard work paying off that we got sick of him. It's easy now to gloss over Craig Kelly's competitive career. At his peak there were jaded whinings over his consistency and whisperings of media favoritism, all of which was bullshit in retrospect. Craig Kelly got to where he is through shrewd decisions, hard work and that ethereal, sublime style.

There is hometown bias, but I say that on a good day in good terrain and good snow, there is still no one who can touch his swooping, flowing drive. There are many now who go bigger; many others who go into crazier places or give more dramatic performances. But in terms of economy of motion, of every minute movement being directed into a perfect, unbroken dance, he is still the one.

Contend that he's washed up. Say he quit while he was ahead and cashed in before he ever had to do anything ugly. Undoubtedly, Craig is a motivated, pragmatic person who didn't want to destroy his image. Certainly he enjoys the creature comforts and low hassle of a paying anti-career, but, on a deeper level, he never really quit anything. And regardless of current trends, he has never quit progressing.

Craig simply took a left on to the road less traveled and redefined progression: the ideal of solitude and powder and moments of simplicity. Whatever he's done is not as significant as what he continues to do.

We were right back then. Craig Kelly has won.

"You pioneered the whole idea of being a professional snowboarder, making a real living off this, then you were one of the first to pull back and make a living as a freerider. Was there anyone you really looked up to?"

"I really wasn't the first one to make money. José Fernandes was the first, and I would've been right in his footsteps, but Bert LaMar came along and he was the second one. Bert and I always, well, maybe it was me more than Bert, but I always had animosity towards him because he slipped right in there at the time without much experience. He won a world championship and got all this fame out of the deal. At the time, I was thinking he didn't really deserve it. But now that I look back, I realize he learned a lot from José.

He was smart, he knew how to market himself. He was a decent rider, but the main thing was his marketing, and I just kind of picked up where those two left off.

What I had going for me was that I was more a freerider from the very beginning. I loved snowboarding and then I got into competition; those guys were into competition from the start. So I had longevity, which took me into the modern era of snowboarding, where there's more money going around with which to make a living. And more media, too."

"Everyone draws the Tom Curren comparison, as someone who was on top of the competition world and then bailed to be a freesurfer. Did his pragmatism ever cross your mind?"

"Yeah, I'm a big fan of his, but I didn't really follow his career path closely. He spent a lot more time getting to where he was than I did. And he competed a lot more than me, I mean he probably hit more contests in one year than I did in my whole career. He probably won more money in one year than I did in my whole career. He went through a lot before he turned. But at the same time, he was getting out of contests at the same time I was getting into surfing and I certainly admired that. I thought it was cool.

It's not parallel enough to say that's why I did it, but I'm glad he did. It probably helped me get to where I am."

"People don't idolize me for my abilities." Craig Kelly

"Have you ever met him?"
"No. Nor do I imagine I ever will."

"How do you deal with [famed North Shore surfer] Gerry Lopez telling you you're a hero of his?"

"Just put it into perspective. I know the things I do well, people don't idolize me for my abilities. More for what I'm doing out there, places I ride, a little for the way I ride those places. It's easy for snowboarders to look up to surfers, and vice-versa. I've been

snowboarding for 15 years and he only started two years ago, so it's easier for him to look up to me. Gerry's an amazing dude."

"Tell me a little about your education. You have a pretty good grade-point average from the University of Washington don't you?"

"Yeah, I think it was a 3.2 or a 3.4."

"What was your field?"

"Chemical engineering. 15 credits to go for graduation. But, uh, it won't ever happen. I could never live in a real city again. I'm motivated to learn throughout my life, and on a daily basis I want to learn but the organized learning environment of college doesn't really appeal to me right now."

"So we won't be seeing a Dr Kelly any time in the future?"

"No. I've always been really long-term goal oriented Going to medical school was a goal of mine six or eight years ago, but now I realize I don't want to."

"You said you want to try to get away from goals. What prompts you?"

"Goals and expectations are the keys to stress and unhappiness in life. Well, it depends on what your goals are and I always set mine pretty high. I've just gotten tired of having these self-applied pressures in my life and I want to live about five or 10 years without any pressures from within. Just let my life go where it may. I'm not there yet. It will probably take three more years before I can free myself from all of that and feel I have no stress to contend with."

"When you pulled out of contests, what was your primary reason?"

"[Long pause] I can't really remember. It's only been a few years, but..."

"Well, what was the last contest you did?"

"I raced the Baker race [Mt Baker Banked Slalom] two or three years ago, but that was more for fun. The last contest before that was the Arapahoe Basin/Body Glove contest a while back."

"How long ago?"

"Ninety-one probably. And at that time – okay, it's all coming back to me now – I felt like I'd done everything I could with competition. I was just revolving at the same speed. I couldn't get any farther. I didn't feel like I was progressing personally in snowboarding. I felt like I could do a lot more in freeriding, and videos were just starting to take off. The only video work I had done was in between contests and it was rushed. I didn't think it showcased freeriding very well. So I wanted to do more and I felt like I was at a point where people weren't even stoked to see me win. It didn't

do myself or Burton any good for me to win another contest, while the video work was much better news. The thrill of victory just wasn't pushing me any longer."

"Goals and expectations are the key to stress and unhappiness in life." Craig Kelly

"Was there any thought of wanting to go out on top?"

Well [long pause], it worked out good that way. I wasn't the champ that year, but I felt strong. I could've won contests at the time. But I didn't want to fade out and be forced to quit. On the other hand, I didn't consciously try to quit at the peak of my career. I was getting a lot of second places that year, but I won the first contest at Mt Baker and the last contest at A-Basin.

"Who was beating you?"

"Randomly, Brushie a lot. Keith [Wallace] beat me. Jimi Scott beat me at Stratton. But they were all really close."

"Did Terje [Haakonsen] ever beat you in a contest?"

"No. He beat me in Alpine events, though. He got second or third at that A-Basin contest, and in all likelihood he would've beaten me in the next contest. And you know what? My plan for the next year, the year I quit competing, was to do, like, three major contests. I was going to do Baker, Stratton and Breckenridge, but I got an opportunity to do some filming right away that kept me busy all year. It was, like, why even show up for the contests? Burton pretty much backed me up on that."

"You were saying earlier you wouldn't want a job in the industry, the usual post-career move. Can you expand on that?"

"Well, the simplest answer is that, as a pro snowboarder, you feel like you're exploiting yourself and the sport a little bit. And after a while it feels a little bit sleazy to turn the thing you love into something you have to do, or to have an entity within you that is separate from going out and having fun. I've gotten away from that right now and I want to keep getting away. I want to get away from tainting my experience with snowboarding and working in the industry."

"Why?"

"Well, first of all, there's the personality trip of the image you have to have to be in the industry. You have to have some kind of act, or whatever, and I just don't want to deal with that. And I don't want to deal with people who have an act, like so much of the industry. I just want a pure snowboarding experience. It's easy for me to say; I'm set up. I don't have to do it. If I was low on money it would be the easy way for me to go and I might be there right now. But I'm fortunate to be set up."

"Although you do have some obligations. I mean, you still do Japanese demos and things, dealing with the media. It's not like you ever checked out altogether.

"No, I never really checked out at all. I just regained control of my schedule. I don't really do Japanese demos anymore, but I do a promotional appearance in a shop in the fall. And I still design boards for Burton. It's in my best interest to go out and do a couple of promos to make sure everyone at Burton realizes I'm still behind their product. And it's not something I'm obligated to do straight for the money. I just like letting people know I'm stoked on what they do for me and I'll put a little work into it from my end. But on a promotional level, I do like three or four days a year at the most."

"Are you a pro snowboarder?"

"I still make money, so I'm a pro snowboarder. I think that's the only definition: If you make money, or not."

"You're an avid reader. When we were in Alaska I noticed you were reading Isaac Asimov, and on this trip you're reading Joseph Conrad. What was the last really good book you read?"

[Long pause] "I think every book I read is pretty good; there's very few I don't enjoy. But the last one was really deep to me [long pause]. Well, I just finished *Heart Of Darkness* today and that was the last good book I read. It frees your mind; there will be thoughts in your mind you don't even know you have and books free those in you."

"What would you say to those who criticize you for drawing a good living off of snowboarding without being a very vocal spokesperson?"

"I think I was pretty vocal when I was the premier guy. Competition was the focal point at the time and I was super into making the rules better, making things better for the riders coming up. I also had a promotional guy I paid for a couple of years to send things to newspapers and help promote the sport. I mean, it was for me, but he helped promote the sport in general. In that respect, I did my thing at the time and now I just ride for fun. I don't even like talking about snowboarding so much anymore. I just don't enjoy the conversation in general, but if a kid wants to talk to me about it, I am certainly open to it. I'm not negative. But I don't really have any goals about working with the media anymore."

"You don't feel like there's any obligational energy between yourself and snowboarding?"

"I don't think I have any obligations. Nor do I think I'm capable of it. I mean, I'm sure I could be one of those announcers on ESPN or one of the other channels. But beyond that, I don't think there's really much I could do."

"I'm a pro snowboarder, the definition is if you make money or not – and I still make money."
Craig Kelly

"What about a mall tour?"

"A mall tour [laughs]. I've already done that. I got sucked into a few of those 'Extreminator' demo stops [Andy] Hetzel was doing and got to take part in those. I did a guest tramp session once. [Laughing]"

"Where at?"

"Ohio, I think."

"Wow. What was your favorite tramp trick?"

"I never really rode on them with my board: I couldn't really even do a backflip.

"Man, you're not as good as I thought. What direction do you see snowboarding going in the next ten years?"

"Things have already turned away from specialization. The freestylers are interested in getting better in the big-mountain environment, and guys who are riding crazy lines on dangerous mountains want to do more freestyle tricks."

"Do you ever consciously think about your riding?"

"I think I try to ride the funnest line. Not necessarily the hardest one, or most dangerous one, or the toughest tricks, but the one that feels

"Well, physical things like action sports. Riding a really good trail on my mountain bike, or snowboarding super-good conditions. On a simpler scale, I'm learning carpentry; it's like learning a new trick on how to put something together and do a really good job. It kind of goes along the lines of just learning for the sake of it."

"Your dad was a big influence early on, wasn't he?"

"He was super-good about giving me advice. He taught me the value of hard work and how it will pay off. I watched him with his moving business and a lot of his hard work and sacrifices and how it paid off. I saw and learned from that, which helped me in snowboarding."

"How do you transfer that work ethic to your now?"

"All the normal things in life – all that comes down to how your parents raised you and my dad taught me not to be a slacker. But in my snowboarding life, I don't know if it really applies much any more. In

the best – the grooviest. I'll do a little spinner every once in a while, but I don't do that too often."

"Out of all your travels, is there any place that really stands out?"

"Yeah, Alaska in general. It's a place where you don't feel in control of your environment. You really have to adapt to the environment, as opposed to most ski areas where you're in control and can be as creative as you want. In Alaska you can only push the limits as far as the mountain might let you."

"We were talking earlier about ski areas and how you avoid them now."

"Just the thought alone of snowboarding, of grabbing my board and sliding down a hill, doesn't exactly grab me and make me want to go. It's got to be either good conditions or a really nice experience, and the nice experience part of it, for me, means not many people around. Maybe nobody else around. Just absorbing a lot of nature, with not a lot of man-made stuff.

So, if the conditions weren't really good, I wouldn't have any business going to a ski

area. Although I still ride some mediocre conditions if I'm at home and I'm going to be gone for a while. If it's my last chance to ride Baker before a trip, I'll go up regardless. I never go out in a big group and do jumps or anything. I think I have more fun in mediocre conditions just going really fast on the hardpack. I don't have any desire to wear hard boots and do the Alpine thing, but I sure do wish I could ride like those guys do on my freeriding board. Like driving a sports car."

"Tell me about The Tao of Physics."

"The Tao of Physics is a really good book. It sort of converges quantum physics, quantum mechanics with Eastern philosophy. It does a full circle on all philosophies combined and ties everything together. It makes you realize even if people have opposite beliefs they are still part of a larger whole and just as important who ever they are. It also make you realize that science and religion are not polar entities with opposite intentions."

"What are the things in life which stoke you out now?"

fact, I'm trying to go the opposite direction and be mellow, let things happen and not be too driven. I just try to ride and have fun without having a reason for it. And along the lines of hard work, there's a lot of days where the powder's awesome and the helicopter does all the work, but there's also a lot of days where the heli drops you off and doesn't come back for four hours and you're hiking your ass off the whole time. It's a work-ethic thing; I feel like I'm doing a job and I want to do a good job of it. Part of it is because I want to get a lot of good runs in and I don't mind hiking for it."

"Let's say the whole thing goes up tomorrow. There's no more money in snowboarding and we all have to go get real jobs. What would you do?"

[Long pause] "At this point, I'd probably do some kind of carpentry, if there was demand for it and it paid well. I like the satisfaction of putting something together, finishing a project, or working on a house."

"If you could change anything about snowboarding right now, what would it be?"

"What probably bums me out more than anything is the rate at which sacred runs at Mt Baker get skied out now.

The rate at which that's changed and how many people have followed somebody, who followed somebody, who followed somebody, who probably followed Carter [Turk], or Dan [Donnelly], or [Jeff] Fulton, or me, into these runs. They just go right at them now, so an average day at Baker gets skied out too fast. I don't blame that on anybody, or hold it against anybody, it's just something I don't like."

"Tell me about your first day of riding."

"My first run was up on Austin at Baker with Fulton. We both had Burton Backhills with water-ski bindings and no highbacks, no edges, no P-Tex. We had the rope on the front of the board and it was a total blizzard. It snowed, like, eight inches the night before, and probably another five inches that day. It was good powder and we just flailed our way down some of the steeper runs.

We absolutely had a great time of it and switched

between using the rope on the end of the board and not having the rope. In the end we decided it was better not having the rope. One day of riding and I was totally hooked on snowboarding; I'd skied twice that year. And that one day was, I felt, the progression and I knew that snowboarding was going to be a lot of fun."

"Was there ever any indication snowboarding would lead to any of this?"

"No, I never really expected anything. But by the time I was 17, two years into it, I knew it was the most important thing in my life. It was the thing which gave me the most satisfaction."

"Is it still the focal point of your life?"

"No, but on a good day I

will think of nothing else than going snowboarding and absolutely loving it. Like more than before. But on the other hand, on an average day or when I'm not snowboarding, it's really just not that much on my mind any more."

> "Just one day of riding and I was totally hooked on snowboarding."
> **Craig Kelly**

"As people grow and naturally shift their attention, would you see yourself ever checking out altogether?"

"I'd love to say I would, I really would. I'd feel more independent if that was the case. But I love snowboarding, I really get a lot of fun out of it. I can't see it so crowded like I can see surfing; I can see that in Hawaii. I can see old surfers there being so bummed on how crowded the good spots have become that they quit because they just can't get away from all the people. But I think

snowboarding always offers another place to hike, a place where you can get away."

"I know you were really into BMX before snowboarding."

"I was as into BMX as I've ever been into snowboarding. Everybody has problems when they're teenagers; I had my share and I always found peace of mind riding my bike. I got really good at it, cause that's all I did. Absolutely loved it."

"How'd you do in BMX competition?"

"In my age group, I pretty much won all the races. So I knew I had potential, but I never figured it out mentally. I'd be strong in the local races and then I'd choke in the big nationals. I got a fourth in one national

race, I was really happy about that. I was about 16 then. I loved to race but the best thing was to ride varied terrain and jump; just doing freestyle in the dirt, I still think that's one of the funnest things in the world that you can go and do."

"Is there anything that scares or really shakes you up?"

"It's really scary to be on a big mountain somewhere and pushing the limits. You check out a line from the machine and it looks do-able, and you try to get out there and then the line freaks you out too much and you say, 'I can't do this,' even just hiking to get to the line.

That happened to me when I was filming with Adventurescope. I got really scared hiking out to this place at Mt Heli sports, and I just turned around and said,

'No, I can't even get out there.' It was between an overhanging cornice and a 400-foot cliff. You had to thread the needle and then get through the tube. That stuff really freaks me out."

"Do you ever worry about the grand scale of things: politics, environmental ruin, etc?"

"No, I really don't. I try to be a good environmental citizen. I do my best to be responsible for myself and what impact I have on the world. On the grand scale of things, I'm a pretty serious guy and I try not to be because the thing that scares me most is to die being too serious. I think that would be the biggest tragedy.

"We were talking about the idea of downsizing, that money itself doesn't inherently bring happiness and that one may be better off owning a few mean-

ingful things rather than having a whole bunch of stuff."

"Anybody who doesn't have money figures money makes things easier. Having the money is not a problem. But then you realize that dealing with money is one of the bigger hassles you have in life: your accountant, paying your taxes – and all of a sudden you realize that even if you're free of debts you still have the problem of protecting your money and making it work for you – well, I'd rather not think about it at all.

"So what is the answer?"

"I think I could make a million dollars if I wanted to work for five years at some project, but I don't think it would make me any happier. A million bucks would be really hard to deal with.

At the same time I've got a nice house in the mountains and I like staying there. I put a lot of energy into building it and making it comfortable. I like the trips in which I go camping with just my van, or sleep on the beach, I think I have easily as much fun with the fewest necessities. Like going surfing in Mexico with just your boardshorts and your board, not needing much else. I think it is those moments of simplicity are the moments of most happiness for me."

"**I could make a million dollars if I worked for five years on a project, but I don't think it would make me any happier."
Craig Kelly**

"Do you ever splurge on anything?"

"Yeah, I splurge on good food. I don't really care about places with upscale service or whatever, but for a really good meal, with wholesome, hearty food, I will pay out cheerfully."

"You don't seem to have any physical vices; I was wondering if there were any secret addictions?"

"Yeah, I'm kind of passionate about surfing and I'll ignore a lot of other responsibilities in my life to do that. Food is kind of like a vice; I'll over-eat, randomly have way too much food to the point where I'm miserable. It's not so much body fat I'm worried about, but I will just get so bloated I can't move or think."

"Do you ever sit there think about how old you are?"

"I figure I'm a pretty good snowboarder for 30. I've been saying that for a couple of years. But no, I don't really think about it at all. I think about the effects of age, like getting sore from playing basketball yesterday. Or if I play soccer, which I absolutely love, I'll be so sore I can hardly walk. But at the time I forget; I just play hard."

"Is there anything you regret?"

"I don't care much about what people think of me, but I regret putting people off. In order for me to be good at competing, it seemed like I had to be so aggro I wasn't fun to be around. I kind of regret that. Things go by too fast to get that serious."

"I'm kind of passionate about surfing and I'll ignore a lot of other responsibilities in my life to do that." **Craig Kelly**

"Are you happy now?"

"Yeah. Not necessarily satisfied; I'm always hungry for another good day of riding. But overall, I'm pretty happy with my position in snowboarding"

"Beyond snowboarding?"

"Yeah, I think I'm still learning a lot about life and where I'm going. But I'm happy. I'm happy to live and ride."

Results and résumé

Craig Elmer Kelly
Birth date: April 1, 1966
Height: 5' 10"
Weight: 165lbs

Videography

- Wrigley's Juicyfruit Gum commercial
- Guinness Book of Records TV Show
- CBS Evening News
- MTV Sports TV program and other MTV productions
- Endless winter; Extreme winter; Escape to ski (Warren Miller Productions)
- The good, the rad, and the gnarly; P-Tex, lies and duct tape (Greg Stump Productions)
- Fear of a flat planet; Board with the world; The smooth groove; Exposed; Exit (AdventureScope)
- Riders on the storm; Critical condition; Gettin' some (Fall Line Films)

Print appearances

- *Rolling Stone* magazine
- *Interview* magazine
- *Ski, Skiing* and *Powder* Magazines
- *TransWorld SNOWboarding, Snowboarder* and *International Snowboard* magazines (Five covers total)
- *Thrasher, TransWorld Skateboarding* and *Action Sports Retailer* magazines
- *Surfer* magazine
- *Snowing* and *SnowStyle* magazines (Japan)

Competitive titles

- Four-time world champion (seven separate titles among freestyle, moguls, slalom and overall)
- Three-time national champion (six separate titles among freestyle, super-G, slalom and overall)
- 1993 winner of the Op Wintersurf (combining surfing and snowboarding)

Other Interests

- Surfing, mountain biking, snowmobiling

Sponsors

- Burton Snowboards, Oakley, Powerbar

Learned to snowboard at Mt Baker, Washington in 1981
First competed professionally in 1985

Career competition results

1985

January
4th; Mt Baker Legendary Banked Slalom; Mt Baker, Washington USA

February
3rd freestyle; Sierra Snowboarding championships; Soda Springs Ski Area, Lake Tahoe, California USA

March
2nd freestyle, 5th slalom, 11th downhill, 3rd overall; Snowboarding world championships; Soda Springs Ski Area, Lake Tahoe, California USA

April
2nd slalom, 5th GS; North American Snowboarding championships; Sunshine Village Ski Area, Banff, Alberta, Canada

1986

January
3rd; Mt Baker Legendary Banked Slalom; Mt Baker, Washington USA

March
7th slalom, 17th downhill; US Open; Stratton Mountain, Vermont USA

1st banked slalom; Pacific West Snowboarding Contest; Hyak, Washington USA

2nd; Aspen Invitational Downhill; Aspen, Colorado USA

1st slalom, 4th halfpipe, 10th GS, 2nd overall; World Snowboarding Classic; Breckenridge, Colorado USA

April
1st slalom, 6th downhill, 1st overall; Le Coupe de Classic; Montreal, Quebec Canada

May
3rd slalom, 3rd moguls, 2nd overall; North American Snowboarding championships; Sunshine Village Ski Area, Banff, Alberta Canada

1987

January
1st freestyle, 5th GS; 3rd Annual Southwestern Snowboarding Association Contest; Wolf Creek, Colorado USA

February
1st slalom, 4th GS; Rocky Mountain Series; Copper Mountain, Colorado USA

1st moguls, 2nd halfpipe, 5th dual slalom, 5th downhill, 19th GS, 1st overall; World Snowboarding championships; St. Moritz, Switzerland and Livigno, Italy

March
1st slalom, 3rd downhill, 1st overall; US Open; Stratton Mountain, Vermont USA

2nd GS, 4th halfpipe, 1st overall; Utah State championships; Brighton, Utah, USA

1st slalom, 1st super-g, 1st halfpipe, 4th GS, 1st overall; Aspen Grand Prix Of Snowboarding; Aspen, Colorado USA

April
1st slalom, 2nd GS, 2nd halfpipe, 1st overall; Swatch World Snowboarding championships; Breckenridge, Colorado USA

December
2nd GS; Rocky Mountain series (race); Copper Mountain, Colorado USA

1988

January
2nd halfpipe, 3rd Slalom, 6th super-g, 7th moguls, 1st overall; Snowboarding world cup, Comp 1; Zurs, Austria

1st slalom, 2nd super-g, 1st overall; Ray Ban Trophy cup (race); Avoriaz, France

2nd halfpipe; 3rd super-g, 4th slalom, 12th moguls, 2nd overall; Snowboarding world cup, Comp 2; Bormio, Italy

1st banked slalom, 1st halfpipe, 1st overall; Mt Baker Snowboarding Championships; Mt Baker, Washington USA

February
1st slalom; 1st freestyle; 1st overall; Willamette Pass Open; Willamette Pass, Oregon USA 2nd moguls; 5th slalom; 2nd overall; US nationals; Crested Butte, Colorado USA

February
1st halfpipe, 8th super-g, 16th slalom, 1st overall; Snowboarding world cup, Comp 2; Lech, Austria

1st overall; O'Neil Banked Slalom; Zurs, Austria

1st halfpipe, 2nd slalom, 1st overall; 490 North Snowboarding championships; Chewelah, Washington USA

1st, halfpipe; Vuarnet Vertical Air Show; Snow Summit, California USA

March
1st halfpipe, 10th slalom, 10th super-g, 1st overall; Snowboarding world cup, Comp 3; Avoriaz, France

1st halfpipe, 1st super-g, 1st overall; US Open; Stratton Mountain, Vermont USA

1989
Halfpipe and overall world cup champion
Halfpipe, super-g and overall national champion

1990
Halfpipe and overall US Pro Champion
2nd; Halfpipe world championships

1991
1st banked slalom; Professional Snowboard Tour of America (PSTA); Mt Baker, Washington USA

1st overall; PSTA; Mt Bachelor, Oregon USA

2nd halfpipe; PSTA; June Mountain, California USA

2nd halfpipe; PSTA; Copper Mountain, Colorado USA

2nd halfpipe, 1st overall; PSTA; Stowe Mountain, Vermont USA

2nd halfpipe; US Open; Stratton Mountain, Vermont USA

1st halfpipe; PSTA; Arapahoe Basin, Colorado USA

1992
2nd; Mt Baker Legendary Banked Slalom
4th overall; Op Wintersurf

1993
1st; Mt Baker Legendary Banked Slalom
1st; Op Wintersurf Boardercross

2nd moguls, 3rd halfpipe, 7th downhill, 9th slalom, 1st overall; Snowboarding World Cup, Comp 3; Stratton Mountain, Vermont USA
7th slalom, 1st halfpipe; World Cup Of Snowboarding, Comp 4; Breckenridge, Colorado, USA

April
1st GS, 1st halfpipe, 1st overall; Canadian Snowboarding championships; Cypress Ski Area, British Columbia Canada

November
1st, halfpipe; Trophie Sun Valley competition; Tignes, France

1989
January
1st halfpipe, 2nd GS, 4th obstacle course, 1st overall; Op Pro of Snowboarding; June Mountain, California USA

2nd halfpipe, 2nd super-g, 10th slalom, 1st overall; Snowboarding World Cup, Comp 1; Breckenridge, Colorado USA

1st halfpipe, 2nd GS, 1st overall; Hoodoo Challenge; Hoodoo Ski Bowl, Oregon USA

1st halfpipe, 2nd slalom, 1st overall; Timberline Challenge; Timberline, Mt Hood, Oregon USA

March
2nd, halfpipe; Rocky Mountain series; Ski Sunlight Ski Area, Colorado USA

Contests
are back!

By Billy Miller

Or did they ever leave? Suddenly, it's the eighties all over again – competition thrives as we all tune in for thrills, prizes, cash and . . . something else . . .

Standing in the starting gate of the Mount Baker Banked Slalom I'm thinking about the competition.

No time for anything else. 29 red and blue gates down a steeply-banked bobsled run 2,453 feet long. The annual Baker Banked is an experience unique to snowboarding.

Participating, that is, *competing*, requires somewhat expert skills and your undivided attention. But every Super Bowl weekend an international field flocks to a dead-end highway just south of Canada like the faithful to Mecca.

Maybe it's the freeriding, or maybe we just love contests. Much as we freeride in denial, the snow jock impulse and the excitement of communal shredding keep us coming back. There used to be the Banked Slalom US Open, a mess of world championships and a smattering of local events to feed the need. Then, in 1991, after four Overall World Championships Craig Kelly dropped the bomb that could have killed contests – at the peak of his career he was foregoing competition to *freeride*.

Suddenly contests seemed less worthy. Why compete? To strive for what? Why spend expensive entry fees to freeze your ass off atop a poorly sculpted halfpipe for one, maybe two badly-judged runs and get, maybe, a T-shirt? That used to be enough reason, but what about all those back-country powder lines where you can make any turn you want?

There was, and probably always will be, racing. And its existence necessitates competition. But when Kelly aimed his star power at freeriding, more of the heroes already there got exposed. His fellow professionals followed and so did we, the

press. First a handful, then a slew of film-makers and videographers documented rider progress. The pro organization went under for its umpteenth time and, suddenly, no one needed to compete any more. Contests sucked.

Everything sort of coasted after that. The US Open and Baker Banked haven't skipped a beat. Some series folded, others remained. Powder and huge kickers ruled the day. Eventually contests followed snow-boarders into Alaskan terrain with the King of the Hill. 'Extreme' contests patterned themselves after the ones existing in skiing. Since it's never so good as when someone sees you do it, judges now grade freeriding performances.

Recently, slopestyle heats and the freeride events caught on. Boardercross, dreamed up by former Swatch VP and creative director Steve Rechtschaffner (for a FOX show directed by Greg Stump), introduced a motocross-like course to boarding *derbiers*.

Then in 1994 the bomb dropped again. After rejecting the International Snowboard Federation's (ISF) bid, the International Olympic Committee (IOC) awarded snowboarding to the Federation Internationale du Ski (FIS), organizers of Olympic skiing. The decision was referred to in *Sports Illustrated* as, ' ... Like having Augusta National Golf Club run a Martin Luther King Day Parade.'

But with that single announce-ment Olympic snowboarding went from 'maybe someday' straight to the

Winter Olympics, Nagano, Japan schedule which we saw in 1998.

After that single stamp of approval snowboarding and its contests were every-where. Now you still have the Banked Slalom and the US Open, plus a couple of world championships, an extreme series, Boardercross, numerous big-air excesses, ESPN's X-Games, loads of events and still your presumed need persists.

There are standardized Pipe Dragon pipes and TV drawing corporate sponsors – Visa, Bud Lite, AT&T, Chevy, Nike. Add in the ISF and FIS (with close to 20 events), World Cups and the Olympic pay-off and now contests are the place to be.

THE CHAIRLIFT: ON YOUR WAY TO THE BIG CONTEST?

"It used to be, if you did contests you didn't get much coverage in the mags." **Barrett Christy**

Know a good agent or personal trainer? Athletes are hiring.

While snowboarding blossomed, contests were the gathering place. Riders would drive, sometimes cross the country, to make weekend start times. Snowboard industry sponsors could scope riders and equipment, contestants could push their abilities, spectators could party down and though it seldom seemed like it at the time, history was made. A scene other than a trade show congealed. I remember in the late eighties thinking contests were truly pro when they ran into the work week – who beside a pro could go?

For US Olympic team member Barrett Christy, that commitment was tested two seasons ago when she entered both Gran Prix events, Freeride, the X-Games, the Vans World Championships, the US Open, the Banked Slalom and was set to go UnVailed in Vail, Colorado but got injured. She earned results across the board – slopestyle, big air and halfpipe. Combined with freeriding skills, she stands out as one of the world's elite riders.

Yet, such a contest schedule was "a few too many," she says. "The year went by so quickly it seemed. But I had fun. If you do well in one, you think you are all cool and it provides incentive. Winning money is nice but there were definitely some days I would have rather been off riding powder. I go because the people there can push me, you can pick up things, see what others are doing. There's so many different

> "I can't do contests. I got too intense. Competitive. Too serious. It's bad energy for me." **Craig Kelly**

events, not everyone goes to the same ones. Snowboarders don't follow a set series. I didn't go by points, I went by the ones that sounded the most fun."

Even when competing for money and contractual obligations, having fun is still job one.

"I'm into it if it looks fun and your friends are there. I don't like taking a lot of time from freeriding," says Shin Campos. He's been pro for a few years but rarely competed. Now he expresses interest, especially in Boardercross, though it is not because of any sponsor pressure: "The sponsors would support me if I wanted to compete and I want to do more, but it is not a prerequisite," he says. "They were stoked that I *wasn't* doing contests."

Indeed most sponsors are now hip to how an unhappy athlete is unproductive, so generally, as long as a pro is doing *something* to promote their goods or name, it doesn't need to be at a contest.

The thing is, contests are fun again. One thing making them more so is the decent prize money that the competition promoters now offer. Few know as much about having fun winning it than Mike Basich, who's been doing both for the last nine years.

"I think the contest scene died about two years ago," he says. "It's a huge thing for European sponsors but in the States they don't look at it as much. This year it's definitely making a comeback. There's a lot of prize money – at least $10,000 for first and $25,000 at a big air in Sapporo, Japan. I'm definitely more into them, they're funner."

Basich adds, "The US Open is exactly the same competition as the Olympics. It's a fun, big thing to win.

"Competing is tougher, there are younger kids with skating experience. It still has a long way to go before the top 40

THE VIEW FROM THE TOP OF THE HALFPIPE.

people are really tough. Right now, the top 10 stick out as tough."

Being on television for real is becoming a prevailing competition concern, but that's a whole other topic. Though his riding's still legendary, Craig Kelly sounds like he's happy with his earlier decision, "From what you say, people are reacting to outside stimuli rather than their actual stoke on contests," he says, while freeriding at Island Lake Lodge. He also acknowledges the opportunity the Olympics provides, "I would have loved to in my time. That's why I'm stoked for the riders who wait through contests. It's awesome to be at that level. But when I can come do *this*. When there isn't enough time to do this … "

"You can't talk shit if you're not putting back into snowboarding as much as you can. Put in what you want it to be. Otherwise it'll be some big, dumb jock. Be loud-mouth, obnoxious – let the kids see you have fun and clown around. We're responsible for the way it becomes."
Tobin Wells

Professionals compete for prize loot, a salary and one of those paperweights the IOC hands out every four years, which can translate into more money.

There are worse jobs, but why compete if you don't have to?
After spending $122 on entrance fee on Mount Bachelor, Oregon's Enter the

RIDING BACK – GOING TO OR BACK FROM A CONTEST.

Dragon halfpipe series, Tobin Wells was told he'd qualified for USASA Nationals. One trip to Big Bear and $200 more later he was third in the halfpipe, third in slopestyle and second overall in men's (older amateur) freestyle. His tangible prize? Three medals, worth $30. He also won a raffled snowboard but gave it to a young bystander. "Blew his mind," Wells remembers. "Just turned around and gave it to him. That made me feel better than anything in a long time."

Those who know him would be more surprised Tobin was *in* a contest than at how he donated his loot to an anonymous grom. After graduating from Northern Arizona University (BA General Studies) he moved to Oregon. While most postgrads fretted over careers, Wells flourished – he has snowboarded and skated just about every day for years.

Why would someone like that compete? "I've been snowboarding so much I may as well compete, it's poking around the different layers and finding something else," he says. "A lot of kids earned their money to go. Worked and saved for it. It was the chance to session with people from all over. Part of the commitment. A good excuse to go skate the Nude Bowl."

The experience ran the gamut of emotions. "It was funny because the stupid

contest made me salty," he says. "Everyone was telling me I won so when I didn't, it was a letdown. I was bummed because I was so caught up in it. Then I was twice as mad at myself for getting salty."

"Snowboarding is a soul sport."
Tobin Wells

The toughest run-ins were with the parents. "They were pathetic," Tobin Wells says of the Nationals. "It's going to become like Little League, and snowboarding's the antithesis of that. Snowboarding is a soul sport. None of the Olympic people care about snowboarding because they're not snow-boarders. It shouldn't be parents yelling and pressure. Not to the point where some kid doesn't want to go up to the mountain."

The back-country will always beckon, but contests may be another place where we get together to prop up what we value most of all: good riding. Of Wells's near win, his girlfriend Sheila appropri-ately sums up: "Tobe did the raddest method out of all of them."

Judging still gets a bad rap, but now qualified people are working to standardize the criteria they use for their sentences. "The judging's getting tighter. If you touch the ground, they'll call you on it. It's more conserva-tive on your performance as a professional, not as a hucker," says Mike Basich. The huckers work against that by hucking harder still. The athletes and judges still tug-of-war over what to

HANDS-ON – BUT IS THIS A LOSS OF POINTS?

LOOKS SCARY?
GOOD RIDES ALWAYS DO.

reward, but now they find common ground in the dialogue.

"I wish some of the riders had to judge just one run in the US Open," says halfpipe judge and former pro Brian Harper.

With snowboarding's Olympic debut a shady memory, one contest truism remains, "The winners get stoked and the losers bitch about it," notes Barrett Christy: "I can win and bitch at the same time, though."

As for me, back at the Banked Slalom, I should have been competing instead of thinking. Day one I took too wide a line on the headwall, ending up just below the gate and face down in fluff. I crawled up around that miserable corner and finished – DFL. Next day, after some rocket wax from George Dobis and advice from Bob Barci, one of the race originators, I improved my time, but so did everyone else. With results separated by microseconds I didn't make the coveted Super Bowl Sunday final.

Though the freeriding was all-time, not making the cut still eats at me. It seems the more we grow up, the more we feel the need to prove our place. *Any* place. Snowboarding contests have grown up with us, but it will always be more fun to win than to lose. Next time, I'll train, reminded of a *Calvin and Hobbes* cartoon:

Calvin: How come grown-ups don't go out to play?

Dad: Grown-ups can only justify playing outside by calling it exercise, doing it when they'd rather not and keeping records to quantify their performance.

Calvin: That sounds like a job.

Dad: Except you don't get paid.

Calvin: So play is worse than work?

Dad: Being a grown-up is tough.

See you next year.

By Jeff Galbraith

Terje Haakonsen

At Home with the World's Best Snowboarder

ncle Hans drives a truck. Explaining the rig, he gestures with the emotive swoops of a painter and smiles after each careful motion. A mossy trucker beard rustles against his chest as he levels his dancing hands. He smiles.

In a small cafe-pub in Oslo, on a spring evening with the sun struggling to set against northern polarity, Uncle Hans enjoys a visit to see his nephew and some guests. He orders up another round and begins more discourse. Fresh beer, fresh topic: soccer. Tense moments of a razor victory are recounted, regional songs are warbled and *bam*! (the slap of a hand on the table, beers jiggling), a winning goal for the home team. Uncle Hans beams, reaches over and grasps his nephew by the scruff of the neck and growls contentedly. They are family at its best.

Uncle Hans lights up a smoke, goes out to his car, comes back with a case of beer, hands it over and bids goodbye. Terje nods proudly, slowly and says, "That's Uncle Hans."

For Terje Haakonsen, such moments of simple comfort and rhythms of home are rare and welcome. The 21-year-old has given up a good chunk of his young life to being the World's Greatest Snowboarder, along with its benefits and burdens, and a few hours with Uncle Hans is his decompression chamber. A voice that cuts through the airports, hotels, contests, photographers, journalists and sponsors and pulls him home – a now almost mythical place for Terje.

Oslo is a terminally middle-class society with a terminal clutter of middle-class boats in its water. Like a software neighborhood in Seattle, Portland or Palo Alto: Volvos, boutiques, manicured playing fields and pricey fast food. Shiny happy people. Crime seems minimal, the streets are clean, urban artwork breaks the cityscape

and a sense of total utilitarian harmony blows through everything. Including the apartment that Terje occasionally gets to call his home.

While his nouveau-riche peers go for Tahoe townhouses or La Jolla four-bedrooms, Terje Haakonsen lives in a modest one-bedroom loft. The kids downstairs listen to Bad Religion, and Terje has, of course, introduced his parents to snowboarding. His apartment contains college-student-who-skates decor: Toulouse Lautrec prints, couch, television, VCR, Madonna videos, the Pixies' 'My Velouria' playing on the stereo, a scant littering of Burton goods and low ceilings.

Truth be told, he lives and tries to exist like

any other good citizen of the twenty-something snowboard nation.

And usually he succeeds, except for the faxes from MTV Sports. And kids asking for autographs in the airport, and taxi drivers in Oslo knowing who he is, and mothers trying to buy the clothes off his body for their children, and Japanese photographers snapping even while he eats breakfast. And European TV reporters who hang around hotel lobbies at contests with their running Spicoli hip-hop-grungy-a-go-go commentary.

Except for these and a few other details, the best snowboarder in the world lives and acts like a million others of his generation from Newport to Narvik. He sleeps late, parties with his friends and skateboards. But then the plane will leave for Denver or Geneva and he will go and reset the world's gauges on what it is possible to do while attached to a snowboard.

Golden child

"Put your hand out," he nods. Palm up, I extend my arm and open my fingers. I expect an object the size and weight of a few coins. He instead releases something so dense it feels as if it could pass through my flesh and fall to the floor. Like Charlie en route to Willie Wonka's chocolate factory, I open my fingers to see a single gold ingot. Terje smiles until he cackles with laughter. He won this and several other gold bars at this year's Red Bull Air and Style stadium launch-fest in Innsbruck, Austria.

"We had to go into a special room at the airport to pick up the gold," he says, smiling like a child who's gotten away with something. "And the guy at the counter looks at (Scott) Needham and me like we're total bums and asks what we want. We tell him we're there to pick up some gold and he just laughs at us. He asks me my name and I told him and then he makes the connection. And from then on it's, 'Yes, Mr Haakonsen. Right, Mr Haakonsen.'" Terje laughs again, shrugging at the gold sausages like he can't explain any of this.

And really, he can't explain any of this. Growing up in small-town Scandinavia, the son of a baker, Terje originally thought soccer was his ticket. Playing on state-level select teams, the halfback competed in an age group above his own and dreamed of charging the field in World Cup victory like his Argentinian hero Diego Maradona.

"We tell him we're there to pick up some gold and he laughs at us." Terje Haakonsen

Winter in Norway is a season-long cultural sports festival. Nordic and Alpine skiing, ski-jumping, ice-fishing and tobogganing are practised as a form of religion, and the Haakonsen family are solid devotees. Here again Terje succeeded at impressive levels of competition, turning the heads of Norwegian skiers. Then, like someone passing Michael Jordan the ball for his first time ever, a friend handed Terje a swallow-tail Burton Performer. He went off to surf some snow-packed hilly farmlands and he hasn't returned since.

At 8.30am in Riksgransen, Sweden, a small ski area north of the Arctic Circle, the telephone rings in Terje's hotel room. Groggily he grasps for the receiver. It is some kid who rides or does something for a snowboard shop in Sweden. His ankle strap is broken beyond repair. Knowing Terje is in residence with a corresponding amount of Burton gear, he has summoned the golden child at this fuzzy hour.

Terje, who many of the media have tagged as a detached, cocky, unwilling star, fishes through his gear and stumbles to the lobby, new ankle strap in hand. While he may not be the in-your-face spokesmodel or punctual for interviews and film shoots, he does get out of bed so some kid can go snowboarding.

Awed into silence

Later that same day, on the mountain, it becomes hauntingly apparent why he doesn't need to have an overt agenda or rock personality. At a perfectly transitioned quarterpipe, with an immense in-run, a small cluster of riders and an equal cluster of cameras, Terje sizes up.

He stomps his board in determined cadence, buckles his back foot, aims, fires and drifts 15 feet vertically above the heads of all who film and gape, grabbing a perfect, swany method drift. He jostles a little, but stomps the landing. The scene is silent and awed.

He is disappointed. "Gotta get that damned landing," he says with a Norwegian lilt battered by English. Dave Seoane, Terje's friend and maker of *Subjekt Haakonsen*, a video documenting the absurdities of his riding, is the first to break the silence as Terje trudges back up the hill. Seoane drops his camera and says slowly, "What I want to know is how that f....er does a 15-foot backside air."

Time Out

Later in the hotel, Terje's ease with the camera stands in stark contrast to his relationship with the tape recorder. I ask a series of questions which feel increasingly lame. He eyes the micro-recorder with increased suspicion.

He suggests we play chess, and quickly rips through my pawns, rooks and knights, cornering my king with light speed. Grabbing the recorder, he begins to mock-interview the interviewer, asking me questions that are invariably lame as well.

Finally, I quit searching and hit him with the obvious. "What would a gold medal mean to you?" He crumples back in the chair, shrugs. "A bigger house." He smiles and laughs the Scando-giggle. "I don't think about it too much. When the Olympics are coming up, I'll think about it a little." He shifts to seriousness, the face that moments ago took me off the chessboard.

There's still a lot of time and still a lot of money. No doubt Terje is deservedly the most well-paid snowboarder to date, and his reaction to the current situation is a pinch-me sentiment.

Childhood camp-outs

Burton, Volcom, Oakley and Reef support him, as do the swelling contest purses stuffed into his backpack in various currencies (once, he said, he carried home $15,000 in cash). Judging by the college-skater apartment, it's hard to tell. "I pay taxes and save what's left. I want to buy a house someday, but I'm not sure where yet. Probably a few houses, starting first with one in Norway. When I'm able to be home more often," he sighs. In the driveway sits a shining black Toyota sports coupe. Terje's managed to get his accountant into snowboarding as well.

It has not always been this way for a kid from the boatless class of Norwegian society. While the Haakonsen family, including Terje's older brother and younger sister were by no means poor, "With three kids, my dad didn't have extra cash to spend on tropical vacations down south," he says. Instead, the Haakon clan would light out on family camping trips to northern Sweden and Denmark, fishing and playing with his 40-plus cousins.

He counts one special relative, his Auntie Ellen, among his favourites. "She lives in Oslo and I would get so stoked to go see her. She lives with this cool Turkish guy named Miten who worked at the beer and soda factory. He'd always buy watermelon, and we'd have watermelon and soda, and he taught me how to play poker. We were never rich, so it's nice for my parents now with less kids to support. It's cool to give back to them. I paid to build a room on their house last year."

He shifts his gaze to the tape recorder, unsure of its presence capturing all these tales of childhood camp-outs. Terje shuffles a few chess pieces, nods and smiles. "I just want to get to a point where I have to travel less and have more contact with my friends at home."

When his mind is clear and the celestial forces are in alignment, there is no one on the planet who can touch him in the halfpipe. However, with a judging criteria that continues to award gymnastic-style holdover tricks from the eighties, Terje stands to lose simply because he charges progressively harder every run, with greater attention to redefining halfpipe riding than to impressing the ex-freestyle ski coaches at the bottom of the pipe.

Were he willing to pump out runs with the requisite hand-waving J-tears and frontside barrel-rolls, there is little doubt he'd win every contest he enters. But he instead opts to rock the house, winning the real contest – the one inside the hearts and minds of every screaming, freezing grom standing alongside a March halfpipe in Stratton. Terje is not just content to win – though he likes that as well – there is a deeper fire born of small-town Scandinavia, a wintry pride, along with a streak of pure Hessianism which drives him to do the thing at hand a bit gnarlier every time. Like one now mythic run at the Mount Baker Banked Slalom.

"I just want to get to a point where I have to travel less and have more contact with my friends at home." Terje Haakonsen

After Terje qualified in first place for his first run ever down the legendary course, Baker's marketing director Gwyn Howat suggested he spin it around. Terje came out of the starting hut fakie and rode to a fourth-place finish in the second qualifier. Of course, he won the final the next day. A year later he skipped the slalom but won the event the following year with ridiculous ease, proving he could be every bit the racing threat if he chose to.

Story time

For the future, he wants to take his technical prowess even higher above the halfpipe lip. "There are a lot of tricks I can do two feet out that I want to take six feet above. Like heel-edged McTwists off a frontside wall: fakie McTwists. I learned a new trick from Daniel [Franck], a Rodeo flip off a backside wall. That's the only new trick I learned this year," he notes. The gap between Terje and humanity has closed a bit these past few seasons, but he's still several levels above anyone else. He credits Daniel and Johan Olofsson for pushing him in the pipe and Peter Line for general freedog inspiration.

The pale Arctic light of Riksgransen, never waxing, never waning, floods the room and again Terje looks quizzically at the recorder. This is a test he shouldn't have to take, it seems. He shrugs. *What is there to say?* Then, lowering his head for a moment, Terje pops up with, "I got a good story to tell. This is about having no money. Right before Daniel broke a few years ago, he wanted to go to the Westbeach contest in BC. He asked if he could borrow some money to go, so I said yeah, no problem. I was supposed to take the train from my friend's house to the airport the next morning; it's like a two-hour ride. I missed the train, and I was supposed to meet Daniel at the airport. There was nothing else to do but call a cab. So I took a two-hour cab ride to the airport for $300. Got to the airport and took a bunch of money out of my account for the tickets and maxed out my card. We scrambled together and had like $50 left.

We fly to Seattle and we have to get to Whistler. We find a bank machine, but the card's still blocked. We knew we weren't going to have enough and we were getting hungry. We bought some food and told the bus driver our story. Finally he says, 'It's getting dark, I can't just leave you.' So he threw our bags in and we got a free ride.

"We get to Vancouver and we got like $15 left, right? We go find more bank machines but my card keeps getting shut down. We had enough to get to Squamish with like two bucks left. I figured we could hitch hike to Whistler from Squamish if we had to. We get out at Squamish and it's dark, there's nobody on the road, we're both 17 years old and we don't have any phone numbers of anyone in Whistler. So I look at Daniel and I'm like, 'You gotta come up with something. Go talk to the bus driver. Start crying, or something. Speak! Speak! Accent! Accent!' I tell him. Daniel's paranoid, it's his first trip ever and he's gotta talk this Canadian bus driver into giving us a free ride. The guy's about to throw our stuff off the bus, and Daniel starts going off, 'We've got friends in Whistler! We can give you the money when we get there!' Daniel's giving the guy the most pathetic look, and finally the driver throws our stuff back on the bus and we go to Whistler. We had a hotel up there already, so we were stoked."

"I used to deal with shit like that a lot."
Terje Haakonsen

Terje laughs honest, clean laughter at this anecdote. "It seems like I used to deal with shit like that a lot. I used to get lost when I was a kid, too." He shuffles more chess pieces, looks out of the window at a passing train and its solitary whistle. "I don't know, what does anybody want?" he asks, finally pulling a complete coup and interviewing himself. "I don't want to lose touch with my friends at home. Less travel and everything would be fine," he nods.

"Want to hear another story?" he volunteers. "About what?" I ask. "About getting lost," he says.

"I went to this soccer game with my family and we're going to our seats. I look back in the crowd and they're not there. I couldn't find them. I figured I'd go to the car and wait there. So I walk around the parking lot. It was a really big lot. I look around and I can't find the car. I'm just this little kid, so I sit down on the grass and I'm crying. Then on the loudspeaker this voice booms out, 'There's a little boy lost and crying in the parking lot. Can his parents please collect him?'"

He breaks up into laughter. A breeze blows through an open window, a sharp North Pole wind subduing the rank smell of snowboard boots and cigarettes. "My family still gurns me with that one," he says. "They'll look at me and shake their heads and say, 'Don't get lost.'"

Skateboard roots brought
a different dimension to
ski resorts – transitions
shaped by human means
into snowboard parks.

King of
the parks

By Lee Crane

just call me 'Champ.'

It was one of those worked days. Complete rot. Overcast, raining, cold and windy. The snow in the trees was chunky pavement, the crap on the runs was boilerplate. If I didn't know better I'd say nature was in a vindictive mood. The few people dumb enough to show up left hours ago. The lifts were desolate. It was just me and the mountain, if you could call it that.

Normally, I'd just screw it and pack it in, but there was nothing going on at home. My girlfriend was still at work and I can only take so much of jacked-up, white-trash families letting the whole homebound nation know how inbred they are on The Jerry-Jenny-Sally-Ricki-Maury-Geraldo Show.

Putting my hands up to shield my face from the stinging rain, I tucked it to the snowboard park. It was empty and ugly. No one had groomed the hits in over a week and thanks to a recent heat wave, most of the good stuff was chopped and rutted all to hell. The highways were bottomless, the sliders all twisted and tipped and someone had kicked the garbage cans into the woods.

I stopped above the first hit and slumped to the snow. A tiny stream of rain was making a micro Grand Canyon past the tip of my board. I looked around and noticed that it was a tributary of the main river flowing right under my butt. So what – I was already soaked. There was nothing Mother could throw down that could possibly make things any worse.

It sounds lame, but as I sat there I thought of an old Foundation Skateboards ad. It had a guy laying in the gutter and the type said something like, "From the gutter the only way you can go is up." Sitting there in my puddle on a pissy day it made sense.

Mass market

Why not, I thought, and pointed my board into the highway to hit the first kicker. I floated a foot or two and slammed on my ass ten feet short of the landing. I suck. Turning toeside onto the spine, I wound up for a shaky backside 360 and landed it. Stoke. At the mini tabletop I was ready, launching and making it to the landing solid. I slammed the brakes, looked back up, and smiled.

> ## "When I suck I like to do it in private – which I guess was why I was here now."
> ## Lee Crane

Normally I hate snowboard parks. I always thought they were dumb. They're packed with the bro-brah crew in their yo-boy uniforms. Most of them are rulers. I don't like looking like a kook in front of people who are dishing out the goods. When I suck I like to do it in private – which I guess was why I was here now. I popped out of my binders, grabbed one of the garbage cans, and stuck it back into the donut hole on top of the tabletop because I'm so New School.

Halfway back up the park I stopped to look back at the course. Snowboard parks are a perfect example of what's wrong with Western society. Streamlining. Mainstreaming. They are the strip malls of snowboarding – everything anyone could want in one nice little package that can be medianized, regimented, boxed, marketed and placed on a

MAN-MADE MAYBE, BUT STILL HAIR-RAISING.

FLYING OFF THE TOP OF A HALF-PIPE

"I was ruler. Period"
Lee Crane

shelf in every store, in every state, in every country on the planet for easy access and mass consumption (see *Just Do It: The Nike Story* by Donald Katz). That's what I'd always thought. But standing there alone, soaking in the rain, I had to smile. This is actually fun. Man-made, maybe, but still hair-raising. Maybe I'd just been a dick all along. Damn.

On my second run I launched off the top kicker, threw the board sideways, and drifted a shifty to the landing. I reverted, hit the spine switch-stance and half-Cab'd it slick. I pulled a late 180 blunt-slide on the trash can and I was ruler. Period.

I made run after run and lost track of how many. Taking my board off I hiked it one more time. While buckling in I swear I heard a loud speaker off in the trees: "Ladies and gentlemen, it's the final run in the World Slopestyle Championships. Getting ready to make his final run is a local unsponsored rider. He's the oldest competitor here today and seems to be a real crowd favorite."

In deep

The roar of the masses echoed through the trees. Shaking off the stress like beads of water, I dropped in. First hit, frontside 180 switch-stance 360 nose slide off the spine. Then a Caballeriel over the gap to finish out the run. The announcer screamed, "Oh, he's gotta be happy with that run. His moves aren't difficult but he's really racked up the style points. We're waiting for the total … ladies and gentlemen, we have a tie. That means he'll have to take one more run for the marbles."

I hiked back to the top to make my winning run. As I sped to the first hit my board rattled and bucked in the highway. I moved my weight back to correct it but went a little too far. As soon as my board left the snow it was obvious I was in deep. The landing dropped away and I felt my back slap down, neck whiplashing, slamming my head into the snow so hard I heard it before I ever felt the pain. As I lay there trying to catch my breath I heard a voice, "Hey, are you okay?"

I blinked open my eyes and before me was a ski patrol woman. "Yeah, why?" I replied.

"We're closed," she said. "I'm doing sweep and I can't leave until you do. That looked pretty bad."

"Yeah, I just blew the world title."

I got up and slid down to the locker room to change and get my keys. In the parking lot I noticed a note under the wiper blade: "Drive carefully, champ!"

Yes, I am the champ, I thought, smiling as I slipped into the car. Ever since then, whenever I cruise through the crowded park, busting my limited repertoire of weak-ass 180s and feeble 360s, I do it with a smile.

'Cause now I know who the boss is baby.

A DIFFFERENT WAY TO STOP.

FREEDOM COMES WITH A SNOWBOARD.

Tom Burt

The man who went 'freeriding' – sage advice from the big-mountain pro who first coined the term.

By Eric Blehm

One snowy day last winter Tom Burt walked into a chalet room in Italy, holding a tattered paperback and nodding his head. Like Tom, the snowboarders inside were passing the time – waiting for a storm to blow through so they could go to work, which meant snowboarding. Tom just stood there, nodding his head and motioning with the paperback. "This is right on," he said. "This is my philosophy for life right here."

The paperback he was referring to was *The Log from the Sea of Cortez* by John Steinbeck. TB found his philosophy in the appendix, where Steinbeck quotes a lifelong friend, Dr Ed Rickets:

"We must remember three things in life. I will tell them to you in the order of their importance. Number one and first in importance, we must have as much fun as we can with what we have. Number two, we must eat as well as we can, because if we don't we won't have the health and strength to have as much fun as we might. And number three and last in importance we must keep the house reasonably in order, wash the dishes and such things. But we will not let the last interfere with the other two."

And Tom Burt doesn't let much of anything interfere with his fun. Not that he is a slacker – he's been working hard as a snowboarder since 1983 and at 32 years old he's built and maintained a reputation as the most focused and deliberate big-mountain rider in the world, flowing exposed lines most riders walk away from. He'll look at a line for a long time, poke around with his shovel and if he says it's doable, it probably is. If he says it isn't, it definitely isn't. On the mountain, he's respected – especially by newbie riders who've moved their freestyling to bigger terrain, with possible severe consequences. TB's presence is comforting. He's the best at his work.

But also the first to admit it's not a real job. He's held few of those: projectionist at a local Tahoe theater when he was 12, and teaching high school algebra after college. Maybe that's why he's so good at calculating his risks and dividing time between commitment and pleasure. *As much fun as we can with what we have.* He has a lot. A supportive family and a little house at King's Beach on the north shore of Lake Tahoe, where he's a fourth-generation local.

There are 18 snowboards hanging from his living room ceiling and each one holds a wealth of memories. They include an original Snurfer, Damian Sanders' first professional model prototype; the Avalanche board TB rode down Denali, a first-ever snowboard descent; his first pro model – a Kemper, serial number 00001; and the Ice Age snowboard he rode down Pumori in Nepal, the highest snowboard descent on record at 23,000 feet. All are reminders of a life rich in experience and proof of how long he's been at this game.

TB keeps his house reasonably in order, but if there's powder in Tahoe, the dishes pile up. If Tom gets an opportunity to up and leave on some worldly adventure they'll sit dirty in his sink for weeks, sometimes months, while he's away. Dr Rickets would understand.

Tom, tell me your heritage as a genuine Tahoe local.
I'm a fourth-generation Tahoe resident – my great grandfather moved here back in the late 1800s.

From?
Texas. He was a Texas Ranger – one of the originals. I still have his hat (laughs). He worked in a paper mill between Truckee and Reno, but he didn't like all the paper pulp they were dumping into the river. He felt it was killing the fish and was probably one of the first environmentalists in the area. So he protested and they fired him and he became a game warden for the north shore of Tahoe and built the house where I grew up. My parents still live there – it's almost 100 years old.

Which family member put snow sliding in your bloodline?
My great grandfather skied for transportation. He built a pair that was like eight inches wide for flotation. My grandma used

to take one out and stand sideways – snowboard on it. My grandma's brother thinks he has a picture of it somewhere. I guess that might be where it all began, 'cause it's definitely in my blood.

When did you make the transition from two planks to one?
In 1983 or 1984. I was actually in college at the time.

And eventually you hooked up with Avalanche Snowboards.
Yeah, me and Jim Zellers, Damian Sanders and Bonnie Leary (now Leary-Zellers) were going to races – to contests. We were the first Avalanche team.

And back then, competitions were the way to go. That's how most people got coverage but you guys took a different path, right?
Yeah, we weren't really into racing and training – you weren't guaranteeing yourself coverage. So we started sending letters to photographers. We'd tell them when we'd be in their area, and they were really receptive, because magazines were starting to request shots of snowboarding.

I made a lot of good friends through those shoots, like Tom Hsieh who started ISM (*International Snowboard Magazine*) and guys like Chris Noble and Larry Prosor.

And your approach with sponsors has been different to most people's – you don't go with photo incentives, just straight contracts ...
Yeah, through my experiences with snowboarding and my background – I guess my track record shows that I'll go out and work – they don't need to throw money at me to work with the cameras. It's a much more comfortable thing to have a flat salary, and it's easier. I don't have to keep track of coverage and neither do my sponsors. I probably don't make as much money as I could if I did get incentives, but that's okay – quality of life, no stress.

You've done really well with snowboarding – do you attribute that success to the way you were brought up when you were a kid?
Yeah, my life was basically poor to start off with, in relation to ...

Money?
Uh-huh – we had plenty to eat, enough to do everything, but my parents didn't have enough for us to go skiing. So I worked and saved money for equipment and lift tickets.

I just learned to be good with my money, not spend it on things I didn't really need. I remember wanting a car, and there was no way my parents could afford a car, so I learned to work on them. I bought my first car for $25 and worked on it. Now I'm 32 and I've owned seven cars, and for all seven I've only spent $1,010.

For all seven cars? You're kidding?
Well, there's more money involved for upkeep and parts, but that's all the money I've spent on car purchases.

So there's always a way?

Yeah, I mean, snowboarding is a relatively rich person's sport, but if someone has the drive, it's easy to be a bum, figure out the scams and make it work without much money. I've learned to manoeuvre around the system without spending too much cash. A lot of my friends say that's what's allowed me to buy a home instead of other things – like some ridiculous car that'll be in a junkyard 15 years from now.

"I was professional snowboarder for three or four years and made about $75." Tom Burt

One of your first big scores was that Juicy Fruit commercial, wasn't it?

Yeah … but I was a professional (laughs) snowboarder for three or four years and made about $75. Whoop! Big money! And then I hooked up with Juicy Fruit in the late eighties and made a good chunk of cash. Then Op sponsored our team and that was pretty good money for the day. But I was only with Op for a year because their clothes were horrible back then, so I switched to the North Face in 1989.

And that's about the time you and Jim Zellers started doing bigger lines, right? A new direction for snowboarding.

And it came from skiing, inspired by guys like Tom Day and Scott Schmidt. When I was a kid, me and my friends were known as the guys not to go skiing with, cause we'd take you to places you didn't want to be.

I wanted to be able to ride everything I had skied in the past or could ski. Now I've surpassed everything I ever did on skis – I'm not sure I could do all the lines I've done on a board on skis now. No, I couldn't, I'm sure I couldn't.

Because of tight lines? Snow conditions?

Well, the narrowness of the lines and the control you can have on a snowboard. You can actually schlep (kill) speed and still be going in a straight line – you can't do that on skis. A board allows you to get in situations where you actually are moving forward, but still maintaining your control in a very tight space. It's not easy to do. You can hook an edge and you're in the rocks. That's another thing I've learned – how to fall, especially around rocks.

When your segment comes on in snowboarding movies people can always expect some hairball terrain. Are you levelling off, or will you continue to do things that surpass yourself?

I don't really feel I surpass myself. Most of the lines I really like are so serious they don't look good on film. Most of the ones that are really fun, where I'm flowing down a chute or some line, look the best on film. The serious lines you don't see on the films, where I screw up or there are sections that are really nasty and I have to slow down and change direction rapidly or stop and traverse around rocks or whatever to get to the next section – those lines don't come off well on film, but they are challenging. They make you work with the mountain.

Most people don't realize how important it is to flow from top to bottom for a film shot. What do you look for in the types of lines we do see in movies?

I just look for something that is pleasing to the eye and looks fun. It depends on the situation, but hopefully I'll see it from afar and maybe from below, and if it's really nasty, I'll hike up it on the edge. Eventually I'll look down it and remember landmarks from all the other angles I've taken in. That's what keeps you flowing.

Your lines always involve exposure – to rocks, couloirs with dogleg corners and double fall lines. And you do them at speed.

Definitely. It's more challenging than just wide open and steep, but I love that, too. Exposure means every turn counts. You have to pull up with the situation – key into what's going on. It allows you to go fast, 'cause you wanna get outta there. When rocks are involved – it just feels natural, it's the mountain. I'm very much in control of what I'm doing, and it doesn't bother me. The speed … it adds to my enjoyment of the run.

A lot of people look to you for advice on which lines are safe. Where'd you gain that knowledge?

In college I was part of a search and rescue team and took some avalanche courses back then with Zellers. So we did study the snow, but for the most part it's been practical experience on the mountain. I've never taken a Level One Certification or anything, but I'd recommend it for most people. I don't go out there to die, I go out there to have fun – so I'm always learning and always in tune. I dig a lot of holes in the snow. I know a lot by looking at slope aspects and by digging down,

> "It depends on the situation, but hopefully I'll see (the line) from afar and maybe from below, and if it's really nasty, I'll hike up it on the edge. Eventually, I'll look down it and remember landmarks from all the other angles ... that's what keeps you flowing. Once there's a track in it, the shot's done." **Tom Burt**

but I screw up. It happens.

You play with your realm of comfort, trusting your gut, your intuition. Nobody knows when it's gonna end – that's the feeling you get when you're about to drop. I know I roll the dice quite often.

When other, less experienced riders look to you for guidance, does it make you uneasy?

I don't want to make their decisions. I won't make their decisions. I don't tell them if it's good or not, safe or not. I'll tell them what the snow is doing, like "it's pretty stable on northwest aspects today" or whatever, but I tell them to take a look for them-selves, otherwise they'll never learn. Everybody has to make their own decisions up there. You're on your own.

Most of your riding now is technical on the ground, with air only to negotiate bad bumps in the terrain. You're the first to admit you're not all that pretty in the air.

Oh yeah, I may throw out a T-bone (laughing), but as you know, well, ricks aren't really my thing.

Your gloves don't seem to touch your board that much.

It depends on the air. Grabbing turns it into a trick and, like I said, I'm into riding the mountain, not for tricks. Where I ride I don't feel I have room for tricks. I'm into landing, sticking everything – no matter how big. No butt or hands in the snow. I have to be 'on it', because if I'm not it could be the end – literally.

Did you ever dream in the mid-eighties that snowboarding would take you around the world?

No. I thought snowboarding would end for me within three years of being sponsored – I thought that the sport would grow rapidly because it was so much fun, and I figured there'd be all these young kids who'd come up and take me out. There is a lot of young talent out there. I've been really lucky to stay in the sport this long. My experience – the years – is what keeps me in it.

How many countries have you visited?

I've been all over Europe – Italy, France, Germany, Switzerland, Austria. Then fur-ther afield there's Nepal, Japan, Mexico, Peru, New Zealand, Canada and Alaska – although it's part of the US it deserves its own mention. And, of course, all over the US as well.

Kow many days are you actually at home in Tahoe in an average year?

(Laughing) I don't know. It depends …

On dirty dishes?

(Laughing) They get real dirty … it depends on the snow in Tahoe. If it's good I'll be there. Last year I was away 220 days.

Crazy things happen in faraway places. You told me about an incredible shit you took in Nepal.

Oh, it was beautiful. Zellers – who, by the way, is the best rider in Tahoe – and I dug this toilet at

base camp when we were going to climb up and ride Pumori. It was evening and it was at least 10 below zero. We had pads for a cushy seat. I was just sitting there in Nepal staring up at these absolutely incredible peaks, Nuptse and Mount Everest, and then all of a sudden the clouds broke and this glowing sunset just painted the mountains red while I was sit-ting there taking a dump (laughing). I'm telling you, it was definitely the nicest shit I've ever had.

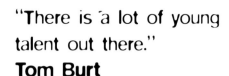

You said earlier you're retiring now, and you'll start working later.

My Grandma is awesome. She's always told me, 'Live life and do what you want to do, because if you wait 'til you're old you'll miss all the things that you wanted to do.

That's what I'm doing. I'm doing every-thing I want now and if I have to work a real job when I'm 65, that's dandy.

You're always talking about mountains you want to ride, and lines you want to do. It's addictive, huh?

Very. I love the mountains.

What's the longest you've ever waited for a line to become do-able – because of snow conditions or whatever?

A long time. There are a couple of moun-tains I've been watching for years. I'm still waiting – when they are ready …

Race
is the place

Alpine riders enjoy rigid discipline.

By Ross Rebagliati, Olympic champion

no comparison: Alpine and freestyle riding are different sports. Riding an Alpine set-up in three feet of fresh powder you can get close to the feeling you get from freestyle, but close isn't good enough. My favorite comparison is like wakeboarding to slalom water-skiing. Close in principle, but really, two different sports.

Whether you ride freestyle or Alpine, the crossover is just as easy. A couple times out on either and no problem. I've been competing for nearly 10 years. The first five were mostly spent on freeriding/ freestyle, and I'd only bring out the long board on race day. Results followed in both freestyle and Alpine competition so I never favored one over the other. But in my first World Cup tour season (1991-'92, after four amateur years) it became obvious that to be competitive in Alpine or freestyle meant one hundred percent commitment to one or the other, and Alpine was the strongest competition at World Cup level.

THE LONG BOARD ONLY USED TO SEE THE LIGHT OF OUT ON RACE DAYS.

There are usually two goals you have your sights set on as a pro snowboarder – winning, and earning enough money to support yourself doing it. Winning and earning usually go hand in hand, but one thing needing to be clarified at this point is that an athlete's first job is having fun and if it's not, you're in the wrong business.

I've ridden about 200 days a year, either training or racing, for about the last five years. I've also contributed to the design of most boards I've been on in those years. Probably around a hundred custom boards have been made for me to enable my board to cooperate with where I want to put it on a course – specifically giant slalom ones. My primary equipment concern has been to finally find a board I like, then get a sponsor to make more that feel the same. Alpine riding to me is on a race set-up making long fall-line carves at high speeds. There is nothing that really has quite the same sensation to it, though a few things come to mind:

Superbike racing – you know, racing high-speed street motorcycles, and I'm not talking from experience. Arcing turns on a superbike has got to feel at least remotely similar to laying down a few really nice turns on your favorite run.

Surfing has that same passion. Safe to say there are similarities that have come through to both Alpine and freestyle snowboarding from the sport of surfing. For me, it's how a surf board can actually carve like an Alpine snowboard. The acceleration you get on a nice wave is the same feeling as dropping in on a really steep section. I could go on and

on with useless comparisons. For those of you who don't know what it's like to snowboard, ride motorcycles, or surf, maybe now you have a better idea. Alpine snowboarding kicks ass!

As does freestyle, of course. Doing something you love is a luxury to be cherished. I love competing – my job. I have so much fun racing, why would I want to quit? I'd like to prove it wasn't just luck in one race and show the rest of the world I'm one of snowboarding's best riders. And I'm really interested to see what races will be like now. Will more people show up? Drawing even 2,000 to a race would be mind-blowing.

Snowboarding has been a part of my life long enough that I've asked even myself what the hell am I doing all these races

ROSS REBAGLIATI
AT HIS BEST.

for? And why aren't I at home in Whistler freeriding with all my bros? But I never come up with a good enough reason. I'd have to say there's an inner drive totally controlling me into pursuing the goals I'd set years ago watching the pros back then realize theirs.

True dedication

Those goals to compete and win have been ignored their share over the years, for reasons that, 99 percent of the time, have nothing to do with the sport. Sometimes it's the politics and other times it's personal. Sometimes sponsor troubles make you wonder if it's really worth it. You really have to want goals badly to realize them. Dedication, hard work, and persistence are words we've heard from teachers and parents since any of us can remember. I would

have to say snowboarding has eased these words into their place. I can't honestly say I've got very many days of real, back-breaking work under my belt. And as if dedication and persistence were a hard one – oh ya – it's really hard to dedicate yourself to ride all the time!

"I made a choice 200 days a year for five years." Tom Burt

But it wasn't altogether easy, either. I had to sacrifice a few things and make hard choices along the way. Two hundred days a year for five years, almost exclusively on Alpine equipment – I can think my board around gates now. And the feeling you get riding super-fast, having complete

control over the board – like it was an extension of your body and you're haulin' ass! It makes everything even out in the end.

As it turned out, the only thing I really wanted, I won on February Eighth, 1998. The outcome of that Olympic Giant Slalom race was a total accomplishment of everything I'd been racing for.

That's how I'm starting to see it. I didn't even think about it before. But now that the XVIIIth Winter Olympics are over I find myself with an entirely different set of goals, simultaneously replacing the ones I had dedicated myself to for so long. The spectacle erased all those days when it was hard to be out there.

The race of life dominates the schedule now. It will be my duty from now on to excel at, and concentrate on an athlete's first job – having fun!

JOINING THE COMPETITION AT THE TOP LEVEL.

Ross Rebagliati

By Billy Miller

The XVIIIth Winter Olympics yielded the genuine article, an authentic snowboarder anti-hero.

Canadian snowboard racer Ross Rebagliati lived two Olympic dreams – one a moment of gold glory before the packed race course, another, a bureaucracy/police/paparazzi nightmare. Two days after shining amidst adverse weather and heavy competition, Rebagliati had his medal stripped in a 13-12 vote because he tested positive for 17.8 nanograms (a thousandth of a gram) of marijuana metabolite in his bloodstream. Rebagliati attributes being over the fifteen nanogram limit (the drug is classified as illegal but not performance-enhancing) to second-hand smoke. While being interrogated and searched by Japanese authorities, his case was heard on appeal and the decision reversed.

Here are small samplings from two TransWorld interviews with Rebagliati – one during the hectic post-race ride down to Nagano to receive the gold medal, the other, in his hometown of Whistler, British Columbia months later. A fierce competitor who was once kicked out of the house for giving up ski racing to snowboard, Rebagliati had to sell his own house to keep racing, barely made the team for missing a qualifier because of shin splints, and won the GS without a sponsor on a three-year-old board. Just as he now enjoys the fame of winning the first snowboard Olympic gold medal, Rebagliati suffers the infamy of what followed shortly after. It ensured history wouldn't forget him, and there was another outcome – when Rebagliati crossed the finish line there would be no going back to fringe subculture for snowboarding.

Before the test

What's your impression of today's race?

It was the best race in snowboard history. They were the closest times – the best riders in the world – all of them competing in the same race from both tours. The first run was perfect. We had sun, the course was prepared perfectly. Then the second run came around with the big ol' fog bank that came in. It was just like, "Okay! Here we go!" But I knew a lot of those guys are fair-weather, purely Alpine riders. I knew for a fact that those guys were going to be really hating those weather conditions and I can do well in that stuff.

Did you ever think the pressure was getting to people?

Maybe in a few instances, but they'll never admit to it. We saw a lot of guys making uncharacteristic mistakes. A lot of the Austrians were favored to do well at this event. Who knows why they didn't, but you can't rule out the pressure the Olympics have.

What can you be thinking after winning?

It hasn't sunk in yet. It sunk in a few moments ago that I'd actually beaten a lot of the best riders in the world but it didn't have much to do with the Olympics. I'm sure the Olympic experience will probably sink in … uh, probably for the rest of my life.

Earlier you said this was a dream come true for snowboarding kids all over the world.

When you're growing up the Olympics are the event to watch, everyone looks forward to it. Since I've been fortunate enough to come through on that dream, hopefully tens of thousands of kids will realize that they can also have the same dream and accomplish the same things I've managed to do. There's a lot of dreams out there but the Olympics are right up there with the best of them. So … yeaaah!

Give us a brief rundown of how you started snowboarding?

I started snowboarding in 1987. My first board was a Burton Elite 155 with three fins on the back of it. Seatbelt bindings. My first pro win was the Mt. Baker Banked Slalom in 1992. That was absolutely my first race, my first season on the pro tour.

You beat Craig Kelly?

Kelly was second. I always looked up to him because I saw him in all the magazines. He was the best, so for me to beat him in the Mt. Baker Banked Slalom was like, "No way, I can't believe it." He [Craig] was three-hundredths behind me. After two runs! He actually got me my first sponsorship with Burton.

Your Baker win was when you still did freestyle?

That was the cross race – I was in my hard boots and plate bindings on a PJ6 [race board]. Kelly was on his freestyle board. After that I started on the World Cup Tour and lost all my sponsors, who thought I didn't have a chance. But I came second in Bormio [Italy] that same year in a GS – one of my first podiums on World Cup Tour. I had a few top-three results but my first pro win on World Cup was when I won the European World Championships in Germany in '94. Then that same year I came second at the Mt. Sainte Anne World Cup in the Super-G and the next week, won the Super-G at the US Open. That put me in second place for the year overall, and was my best season so far. I've done well in other events, but that's the highlights.

What will you remember about today's race?

It's hard to believe. I get little moments of it. It's not that I actually beat those riders but I just … today I beat them. That's the coolest part.

Where will you be next year?

That's a good question, I think it really still hinges on the TV. What's the point of having a sponsor if you're not getting any exposure? But it's hard to say what's going to happen, it really is. I've got a goal, I've never been ranked first in the world. I've been second, and that's good but as soon as I can win the overall title for one year then I'm going to start racing more for money than for the title. Wherever the big events are. It could be different, too – golfers get paid money just to be there. So do the ski racers, they get paid just to show up at the race. I think when it gets to that point that will make it a lot easier on the riders. You know Terje didn't want to

come to the Olympics because he was so hardcore but he can afford to. He knows he's the best, everybody knows he's the best. He doesn't really need to win the gold medal for that to change. He doesn't really have to be at the Olympics if he doesn't want to be. If he doesn't consider it a loss then it's not a loss. Guys like that can do whatever they want because they can afford to, where guys like me have to play the game more. I'm not above everybody else like he is. Maybe now I am [laughs].

After the fuss

A lot has changed since our car ride.
Yeah, I know. In that car ride I was just trying to get a grasp of all the things that were racing through my mind. Am I going to make a thousand, or a million, or a hundred million?

You got the key to the city [Whistler], you don't have to pay taxes ...
No.

Your own run ["Ross's Gold" on Blackcomb mountain].
Yeah.

Free lunch and dinner.
Mambo's and The Tratorilla. I got some land on Green Lake here in Whistler, it's got an epic view of both mountains. It's the only lake in Whistler you can water-ski on and have float planes. I'm actually thinking about getting my pilot's licence and getting a float plane. Be able to fly down to wherever and just surf. Come home, land right by the dock.

You're going to build a house up there?
My goal is to own the land outright, then I'll build a house a few years from now. What I'm going to do is get a big ol' motor home—[Shaun] Palmer would be proud of

it, and live on it until I can figure out where I'm going to put the house and can pay for it.

You have other places in town, right?
I've got a nice little condo on the golf course, 2,100 square feet, then I live in this tiny little one that's 500 square feet. That's good for me, I live by myself. Usually I hang out with my friends anyway, it's not like I'm home that much.

Do they [friends] treat you different?
Oh, exactly the same. Except I went to the Los Angeles/Vancouver hockey game in Vancouver four weeks ago with two of my good friends. I ended up with a standing ovation from everybody, it was sold out. They had to quarantine off our area with security. Everybody in the stadium was moving around to my section to get an autograph. I'd already been exposed to that a couple times before so I wasn't too blown away. My buddies were really blown away. That was their first experience, in Whistler you don't really notice it except for here and there. When you get 30,000 people at once, and have to have a police escort out of the stadium before the game ends, it's kind of a trip.

There's one level to winning a contest, but what happened to you, that's another and they're not really related. The circumstances aren't important, it's what people remember.
That's right. When I won people were stoked and probably would have been just as stoked after that happened. But after the controversy, I think they just saw me again. Most people are just like, "Oh, there's Ross on TV again." It ended up being a positive thing for me. It gave me an opportunity to be myself and just show people ... they saw we're not all idiots. I'm not saying I'm a genius but ... it's like winning twice. A unique thing.

Do you think the race raised the possibilities for Alpine?

I think it did but the industry doesn't want to admit it. Definitely it did in countries in Europe who are more Alpine-oriented. I know for a fact snowboarding, and particularly Alpine, is lot more popular than it used to be. Especially with young kids – 10, 12 year olds – who used to ski race. They want to start snowboard racing. I heard that from a lot of parents. But the industry still feels, and rightfully so, that any money they pay to Alpine just comes from freestyle sales, which is true. But a company doesn't have to produce a board that's for sale. Any company can make a big Alpine board and if a guy is winning that just means all their boards are good. If someone wins a race in an F1 car, you aren't going to be able to buy one, it really just means that Ferrari kicks ass.

Did you think there was any stigma, that what happened to you may have made companies reluctant?

Within the snowboard industry? I don't think that affected anybody. I think the main thing as far as politics goes is the fight between the federations [FIS and ISF]. That's still an issue. I know that Jake [Burton] isn't too impressed with the Olympics. Of course his company didn't podium [in the GS] so that didn't help him. I think it's still going to be an issue in the future. I try to stay away from it and do what I want.

What's your feelings on what you had to go through?

I was stoked it happened to me and no one [else] had to go through that. I think they [the IOC] were a little confused about what to do. Probably the IOC wanted to make an example of me. And I think they did. They broke the law, released confidential test results. I had the option of taking the IOC to

court for millions of dollars. That's just not my nature.

You got put through the ringer.

I won. I was tripping out because I didn't know what to think. I felt like a loser. I did not want to be me. I wanted to move down to South America and not come back. I defended myself in front of the panel of arbitration and the medical committee. I

have to live with that forever. It put a damper on being the first medal that they'll never know. I won – without bringing up that I tested positive. My threshold is a lot higher. You can't hurt me – or snowboarding. Not anymore.

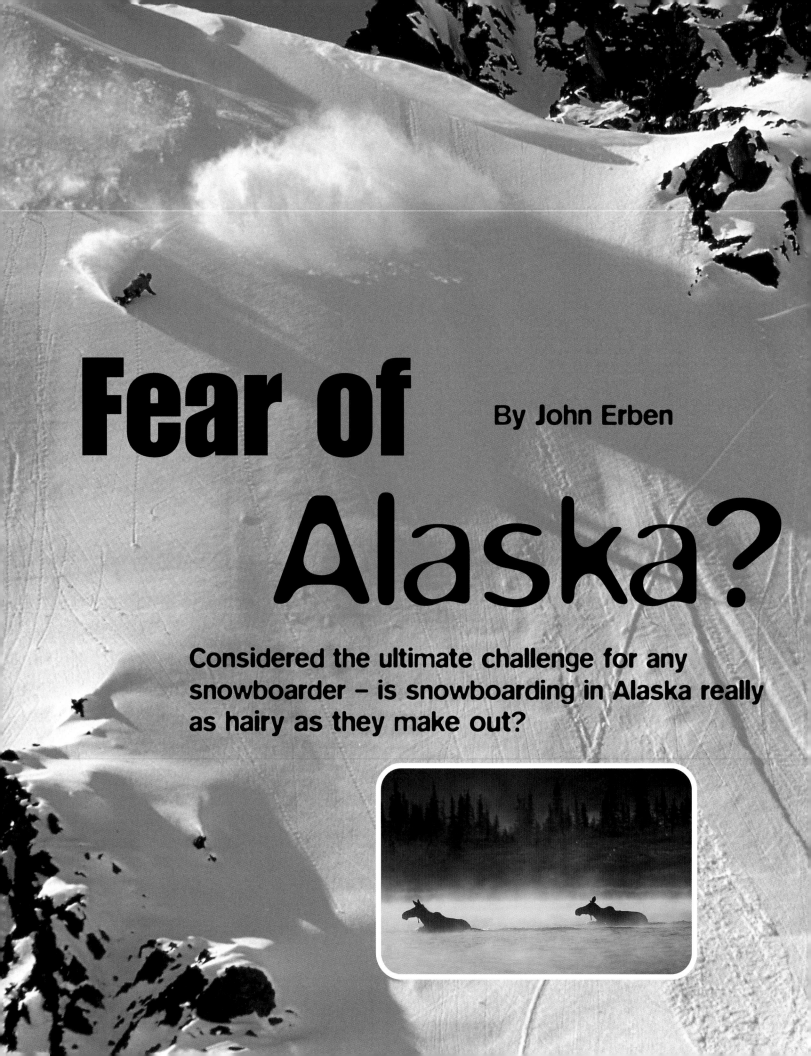

Fear of
Alaska?

By John Erben

Considered the ultimate challenge for any snowboarder – is snowboarding in Alaska really as hairy as they make out?

Part One

the freeriding state's most frequently asked questions

THE WONDERFUL ALASKAN WILDERNESS.

Once upon a time, Alaska seemed almost like another country. The locals referred to anywhere else as 'outside' and spoke of going down to America when they had to go out for sun, surgery or shopping malls. But now, thanks to oil money, fast-food franchises and satellite dishes the world has come to Alaska.

Nowadays, Alaska is a post-industrial consumer wasteland like the rest of America, only with more snow and bigger mountains. Still, that wacky Alaska mystique lives on and inspires wonder. So let's start with the question that everyone asks first.

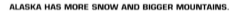

ALASKA HAS MORE SNOW AND BIGGER MOUNTAINS.

Is pot legal in Alaska?

No, but possession of under four ounces used to be okay as long as you didn't sell it or drive after consuming it. Then in a 1990 state referendum 105,263 Alaskan voters (54.2 per cent) got marijuana possession recriminalized. Still, 88,664 Alaskans (45.7 per cent) voted for marijuana.

And 75,721 Alaskans (38.8 per cent) voted in Wally Hickel as governor, quickly prompting a classic bumper sticker to note: 'Pot got more votes than Hickel.'

Alaska is like the rest of America now, in that the police don't really care about marijuana possession unless it occurs in conjunction with some other crime, like being a teenager.

Is Alaska real cold and snowy?

Yes.

ALL ALASKANS WORSHIP PILOTS A BIT.

Is it true there are hardly any women in Alaska?

An old-school proverb maintains that for a woman in Alaska, the odds are good, but the goods are odd. There are tons of guys, but they're all tweaked.

That equation's second part remains true: most everyone here is psycho. But in towns like Homer you can actually hear women complain about the lack of guys. Sure, you still see T-shirts that read 'Enjoy Valdez, honey, 'cuz when you leave you'll be ugly again', but really the local ratio doesn't seem much different in Valdez than in Jackson Hole or Whistler, BC (British Columbia) or snowboarding in general. The current ratio for the whole state of Alaska is 109 men for every 100 women.

The main reason people think Alaska still has an oversupply of brawny back-woods guys is that TV shows and magazines like *Alaska Men* continue to feed outside stereotypes.

Didn't Alaska once belong to Russia?

Yeah. Russian fur traders landed in the late 1700s and began to decimate the Aleut, Eskimo and Indian natives with guns, alcohol and disease. In 1867 Russia sold Alaska to the US for $7.2 million, or two cents an acre.

Not everyone was happy with the deal and a few people still haven't gotten over it. When I moved to Alaska a few years back, Glasnost was going off in Russia and old-timers here were getting all worked up about it. If we were still part of Russia,

some of them told me, we'd be free.

Of course, that's both wishful thinking and living in the past. A truly progressive course would be for Alaska, British Columbia and the Yukon territories to join together in a vast freeriding republic and ram the rest of the US and Canada right down Mexico's throat.

Doesn't Alaska pay people to live there?

Sort of. State residents get what is called a Permanent Fund Dividend (PFD) check

ALASKA RIDING IS SUPER HAIRY.

PRICES ARE HIGH, BUT THE SNOW IS FANTASTIC.

each year. Better yet, the checks come out in October at the start of the riding season.

The bad news is that the Feds tax the PFD checks as straight income. And back taxes, child support, student loans, etc. may also get deducted before you see any money. So, while on paper every Alaska resident got about $1,100 in 1996 from the state, in practice most of us ended up with just enough to buy a few six-packs at AK prices.

Is the riding there super hairy?
Yes. The scale is immense, the exposure is terrifying, the locals are savages and the weather can be more brutal than you thought possible. If you're stupid, you will die. If you're not, you still might.

Will riding the tougher areas in America prepare me for Alaska?
Not really.

I heard that Jerry faked his death and moved to Talkeetna to play bluegrass. What's up with that?
Get it straight, Moonchild. Jerry is dead. Jerry is off the bus. Jerry is taking the big dirt nap. So don't go truckin' up the Al-Can Highway in your micro-bus, trailing clouds of glory and groovin' on the shitty live tapes you traded Saffron and your shitty old live tapes for. The Canadians are sick of seeing you tie-dyed pukes playing hackey-sack in the dirt to 'Tennessee Jedi' next to your broken-down vehicles and they can't wait to give you all hockey stick enemas.

Whoa! Hang on. Sorry, I was bummin' hard for a second there, bro. Hey, the big nurse tells me that Jerry is really hanging in Antarctica! Really, like follow him there now, man! Further brothers and sisters!

Are there a lot of weird cults in Alaska?
Nah, mostly the usual ones – Deadheads, Mac users, Amway people, survivalists, New Agers, salmon sniffers, telemarketers – but most Alaskans seem to worship pilots a bit, and rightly so. Without bush pilots this state would never have gotten off the ground. Alaskans use planes the way New Yorkers use cabs. Pilots make our lives better and make our dreams real.

Most of the photos on these pages exist only because some highly-skilled, underpaid helicopter or plane jockey busted his ass to get some riders, a shooter and their gear to a mountain top that they could never reach on their own.

I worship them too, so every year I give my Permanent Fund Dividend check to the local helicopter company as a deposit for next season's fun.

"Alaska rules because there are no rules?" Isn't that how the saying goes?
That's the saying alright, but it doesn't apply anymore. Take Anchorage (please). Last year a couple of little Ayatollahs on the city council rammed through a curfew for those 18 and under. The voters or the courts will probably overturn the curfew, but now roughly half the teens in the state have a police-enforced bedtime.

Or take Valdez, the alleged home of the extreme. Valdez decided their one rope-tow ski area wasn't worth keeping after a drunk, 15-year-old skier crashed there and paralyzed her legs. Her parents then sued both the city and the liquor store that sold her the beer. The city settled out of court and closed the area.

Or take Juneau, where a current hit bumper sticker proclaims, 'Make welfare as hard to get as a Juneau building permit.' For two years one local boarder had lived in a teepee in the woods off the ski area access road. In summer 1997, while he was commercial fishing, two state Fish and Game agents evicted his caretaker and burned down the teepee.

Or take the whole state. Less than one percent of Alaska land is owned by private individuals. The rest of the land is controlled by the Federal Government and, well, I don't have to tell you that the Feds rule on the rule thing.

So, yeah, Alaska has rules. Alaska has lawyers too, but all the good ones work for Big Oil. The remaining lawyers either live off the government and/or inflame petty domestic disputes. Recently a rural homeowner successfully sued the neighbors over their barking sled dogs.

So all this Last Frontier stuff is just empty hype?

Fortunately not. Alaska may not be snowboarding's last frontier, but it's the best frontier we have on this planet. Sure it has limitations: expense, weather, even rules. But once you get out beyond Alaska's few cities, the main limit is your imagination.

Every year people say that the scene in Alaska is worked, but every year riders use helicopters, planes, snow machines, snowshoes, split boards, crampons and boots to open new terrain. Ordinary snowboarders can still make first descents here and the super-pros have the slickest array of terrain and the best snow conditions on Earth to play with.

THE MAIN LIMIT IS YOUR IMAGINATION.

Alaska stories

**Jeff Galbraith on Yakutat,
April 1995**

"It was kind of decadent, but a bunch of us flew from Juneau to Yakutat to surf for eight hours one day. This local guy, 'Brando', was going to get us a Suburban. We got to our meeting spot at the marina. Brando and the Suburban weren't there, so we went to his apartment. It was 11am and we pounded on the door. Finally, Brando comes out and goes, 'Wow, hey, I really partied last night, man.'

Temple (Cummins) and I walk in and there's a photo of Ace Frehley and a bottle of cough syrup on the coffee table. He got us the Suburban though, and we drove out to the point. The surf wasn't that good …

One the way back, the Suburban got a flat. By the time we changed it we had 30 minutes to get to the only plane out that day. Then the spare goes flat and spins off as I'm backing off a snow patch.

We put the first flat back on and I drive off at about 20mph. I started worrying out loud about missing the plane and Savard, one of our gang, goes: "Hey, I used to drive a logging truck with a flat tire all day in BC!"

"The guy was face down with the back of his head out of the snowpack."
Jim Zellars

Savard took over driving and we did 50mph on the flat for seven miles back to Yakutat. We went to the Chevron station to return the Suburban and I go to the guy there, 'I bet you've never seen this before.'

He goes, 'Oh, yes I have,' and he shows us their Wall of Shame. It's full of Polaroids of wrecked Suburbans with handwritten captions like, 'No, we weren't drinking.'

We just made the plane."

FAMOUS FOR SNOWBOARDING CONDITIONS – AND
FOR AVALANCHES.

"I just got knocked over
when the avalanche hit
me." **Sean Tracey**

Laird Hamilton had dropped (into the chute) and set off a slide on his first turn. I could have gotten out of the way), I just wasn't experienced enough.

I got spin-cycled like I was in a wave, only for longer. It seemed like an hour, but it was maybe a minute in real time. I came to a stop and my upper body was a few inches under the snow. I was thrashing because I was in a panic and hyperventilating I broke out in a few seconds. There was snow packed in my nostrils, my ears, my goggles and my clothes. I sat up and an aftershock wave of snow hit me and carried me along for another hundred yards.

Later that afternoon I was in the bar at Tsaina Lodge and Chet (Simmons, the helicopter pilot) comes in and says, 'Let's go.' I figured that if I didn't go back out then I might not go out ever again. So we flew up and did Dimond."

Bruce Griggs on Mount Dimond, Valdez

"It was 1992, the year of the first snowboard extreme contest, before Valdez got over-run with maggots.

Chet dropped us on top of Dimond. Tom Burt, Kevin Andrews and John Gute traversed around to the backside. I was behind them on the traverse, about a foot above their tracks, 40 or 50 feet below what looked like a knife-back ridge. I was cruising along, looking below me down the east side of Dimond, a big open face, about 4,000 vertical straight down.

I heard a noise and this crack shot out in front of my board. I thought it was cutting out below me so I cut uphill. Then I realized it was the whole top of the mountain falling away from me. So I jumped back downhill and landed on my butt below the

Jim Zellers on Denali and Ruth Glacier

"One year Tom Burt and I were climbing on Denali for a snowboard descent. We sat down for lunch and we saw three bamboo ski poles and a fur jacket collar frozen into the snow. The guy was face down, with the back of his head out of the snowpack ... he'd been there for a few seasons.

Another time, Tom, Bonnie (Leary-Zellers) and I were camping on the Ruth Glacier (in Denali National Park) in a valley a half mile wide. We were going to climb a peak and leave at 7am, but Bonnie's contacts weren't working. Tom and I are just fuming. It's 45 minutes later and we're still waiting, so Tom starts out. Just then, this huge serac falls way above us and a 200-foot cloud rolls across the glacier where

we would have been if we had been on time. We would have been toast."

Sean Tracey on Stairway, Valdez

(This was back in 'The Juan & Richie Days' about 1991, when Juan Gomez and Richie Fowler were the heli-boarding pioneers in Valdez. It was the third helicopter run ever for Tracey, then an Anchorage skate rat.)

"We were at the chute on top of Stairway. I was second down, after Cliff (Swett). I got out of the chute and was on the face below where you can open it up. Cliff was at the bottom yelling at me. I thought he was going 'Yeah!', but he was trying to get me to traverse away. I didn't even hear it, I just got knocked over when the avalanche hit me.

fracture. I watched the top of the mountain fall away.

I was kind of in shock as what felt like two giant hands grabbed me and pulled me up off the crack. I got sucked over the top by a vacuum as one of the main chutes on the front of Dimond fell away. I fell off a 12-foot fracture and landed 180 degrees around on my butt and board on a little rock pinnacle, because the fracture had ripped down to rock.

I remember looking at my Doughboy Shredder with the skeleton face dangling off probably an 80 degree rock slope and below it this avalanche was going off. The top 3,000 feet of the chute ripped out and it went down to the valley between Python and Dimond, then a half-mile down the glacier and around the corner.

"A chunk of ice and snow broke off about 20 feet from me." Bruce Griggs

The guys were on the other side waiting for me because I had the camera. They couldn't see me. They heard the rumble of the avalanche, but they thought it was a jetplane just going by.

Right then Chet is flying up the glacier with Jim and Bonnie. Chet gets on the radio and goes, 'Huge avalanche, is everybody okay?'

I told them on the radio I was on the fracture, just below the crown. Chet told me to stay there, and I'm like, no kidding, because my back's to, like, a 12-foot wall. So I'm waiting on the heli and they can't see me because of all the rock. I wave my hands and they spot me.

Chet was hovering close and a chunk of ice and snow broke off about 20 feet from me and freaked me out. I took my board off and chucked it over the top – luckily it landed bindings down. I kicked hand and footholds in the slope and climbed out. I got out quick, in about two minutes, after lying for about 10 minutes on the fracture.

I get out and I'm laying on the snow, swearing, and Tom Burt comes over the hill yelling, 'What's taking your fat ass so long? Jesus, why don't you learn how to snowboard? Can't you traverse? Why isn't your fucking board on? What, are you having lunch?'

I go, 'Come here.' He crawls out and looks over the fracture and he's like, 'Oh ... never mind.'"

SNOWBOARDING DOWN A VALLEY IN ALASKA.

Whether riding to show up the competition, advance your gender, or simply shine – the point is, enjoy yourself.

By Kennedy

The mother
of sports

personally, I think our mothers had a pretty raw deal. They were expected to live with harder work and diminished profiles without the ability to let loose and have a good time. They were the keepers of schedules, lovers of housework, teachers, semi-professionals, plus all things maternal wrapped into one. Whatever tasks they took on – the child-rearing and all the chores – that was supposed to be the fun part of their lives, ideals from which they rarely strayed. Even the feminists were too serious. Burning bras? Gloria Steinem? Idealistic perhaps, hardly fun. I saw Gloria Steinem at a Madonna concert. She looked bored.

We grew up hearing our mothers mumble dissatisfaction under their breath, but a new generation of women sort of decided, "screw that!" We want out. We want fun!

The first time I went snowboarding I felt leveled by all these new emotions – crashing, laughter, heckling – freedom! It was a pretty good day. I laughed to myself when I'd fallen for the 600th time thinking, "My mother never would have tried this!" In fact, when I called her later that day to tell her how I tried something new called snowboarding she made a funny screech in the back of her throat and told me how dangerous it was. Anything my mom found dangerous has, in the past, turned out to be a good time, so I decided to sign up for a session at Craig Kelly's World Snowboarding Camp in Blackcomb, British Columbia. I heard they had bears.

Before camp started I sat in the Seattle airport scribbling anxiously in my journal, "... What was I getting myself into? ... What if they make fun of me? ... What if it's all pimply-faced teenage boys in baggy shorts? ... What if I'm the oldest one there? ... " I wasn't the oldest one there, but all the pimply-faced teenage boys in baggy shorts took great pleasure teasing me every chance they got, at least when they weren't singing about poo.

Camp was a rigorous seven days of stretching at 6:30am, breakfast at seven, shit talk and bragging on a bus ride and up three chair lifts from eight to nine, and halfpipe/snowboard park from nine until it rained or everyone got lazy and rode down, which was usually around 2:30 or 3:00pm. When we weren't snowboarding the boys were content watching it on video until 6:00pm, which is when they'd switch sports and go to the skatepark. After dinner, slumming and shoulder-tapping in Whistler Village, the hooligans would wander through the driving range stealing golf balls to throw at cyclists and moving cars from 9:30 until 10:15pm. This was fun if nothing else.

In the middle of all the chicanery and arrangements I had acquired a cute nickname on the hill. All the coaches and campers called me 'Maggie Simpson,' from the TV show that could hold their collective attention like nothing besides sliding down a slope of snow. And the girls forged their own special bond – not the kind where you read Maya Angelou to one another and sync up your periods, the kind where you realize you're in a unique situation and had better all stick together and learn, since the odds around you have you greatly outnumbered.

There were fifty campers in the session, five of us female, none of us spectacular, although there was a young girl with much promise and style who rode with her brother every day at a small hill outside Chicago, Illinois. Her name was Paige and she wasn't afraid to try any trick or ride with the aggressive abandon of a guy. All of us tried to ride like the boys.

DANGEROUS; WELL. FUN – YOU BET!

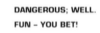

YOU CAN PICK OUT A WOMAN RIDER.

Snowboarding was hardly new five years ago, but there seemed to be this unspoken rule that girls rode, dressed and generally acted a lot more masculine than, say, tennis players or supermodels.

I was used to the corporate environment at MTV where the girls wore short, cute skirts and preened in front of the mirror asking, "Do I look fat?" ("Yes", was a common reply) and behaved in a more distrusting and cut-throat fashion. Here at

CHECKING THE
WINNING TIMES

snowboarding camp the girls were supportive and genuine, a lot less college sorority-like. A lot more fun. The scene in snowboarding at the time reflected what we were going through at camp. The girls who were really into it had learned at a young age from their brothers, or they rode with their boyfriends every day, determined to outshine them.

Playing by rules

It was easy to see why the girls exhibited a strong male influence. They existed in a largely boyish zone and were determined to fit in, even if it meant playing by the boys rules. This never caused anyone personality conflicts or socializing disorders. In fact, we all seemed to benefit from not having to share the tiara. Paige was certainly sweet and polite, and though it naturally gravitated to her, she loved sharing the spotlight with the rest of us.
Just like a snowboarder.

WATCHING THE WOMEN AT EAST U.S.A.

"We want out. We want fun!" Kennedy

The first proper snowboarding exhibition MTV held was in 1994 at Snowmass, Colorado for the taping of a show called Mt. MTV. A lot of great pros showed up including Terje, Bryan Iguchi, Shannon Dunn, Tina Basich, Michele Taggart, Todd Richards – you know, the superstars.

Pro rider Jimi Scott designed a long pipe with a really steep pitch and huge walls, then gave everyone stink eye through the yellow lenses of his glasses before each run. The cameras zoomed, the fans were breathless, the pants were baggy – it was magic. The big neat-o trick women were doing that day was backside 540s, but the guy's tricks were a lot bigger and more technical. It gave way to the most nauseating phrase a professional female athlete can hear, "She's pretty good ... for a girl."

Maybe that's what sparked the girlie revolution that began shortly thereafter. In lots of ways girls had had enough of playing second fiddle. They wanted to compete and excel. Tina Basich and Shannon Dunn started a clothing division called Prom that unashamedly blew a kiss like a whole new side of snowboarding fashion all about women. It didn't feel like a fluke or a trend – the pink and baby blue, the cat-eye glasses, the furry coats – this was a Pepto Bismol parade of women who loved what they did but needed their own imprint of style and substance. Both girls had their own pro model snowboards (Tina for Sims, Shannon for Burton) designed to feminine specifications and they quickly became two of the most popular boards on the market.

In addition to the image and equipment, riding talent flowed like a gusher. Like over-all champions Craig Kelly and Bertrand Denervaud, Michele Taggart could dominate the halfpipe standings just as easily as the giant slalom races. She proved to be a well-rounded, tough competitor, yet sweet as a slice of shoo-fly pie with blackberry sauce. Suddenly it was a new sporty horizon beckoning more women to join.

People couldn't get enough of women in the halfpipe, at big-air events, in the magazines or in person. The ladies had arrived.

But what separated the women from the girlie-girls this time was talent. Instead of the typical, "She's okay for a yada-yada", the boys were gawking from chairlifts. "Holy shit! She rips!" And thanks to cute pants, jackets, bibs and baby doll T-shirts, there was no mistaking the gender. Watch your ass Helen Reddy.

Before athletes ever arrived in Nagano, Japan, the buzz over snowboarding's inclusion in such a mainstream event as the Olympics was deafening.

"The ladies had arrived." Kennedy

For the men most had decided early on that Terje would take home the gold followed by Todd Richards and probably Daniel Franck. Since Todd was considered the only lock on the men's team, the US speculation surrounded the women – Michele, Shannon, Tina, Barrett Christy (or 'Christy Barrett' as announced during the Olympic halfpipe), Carabeth Burnside, Tricia Byrnes, Aurelie Sayers – the field was vast. Too much friggin' talent!

Medal promise

Nagano fever swept the Mt Hood summer camps in 1997 and, to a lesser extent, Craig Kelly's camp. Riders pushed their abilities, 'training' for the first time.

All that momentum women had been building in prior years triggered an absolute explosion. Men seemed to have reached a

SHANNON DUNN, ON HER BURTON DESIGNED SNOWBOARD.

plateau on their new tricks but the sky was opening for women. In a pre-Olympic interview I did with Shannon Dunn for CBS she denied any special training for the Olympic Games. Oh really,

SHANNON DUNN

Ms. Dunn? Then how do you explain those 720s you been doing lately? Everywhere, the riding was nuts.

For all the resentment that being drafted into the Winter Olympics has caused snowboarding, the benefits are visible and irreversible as far as women's progress is concerned. Three 'Grand Prix' events were the main selection process for the US Olympic Team. For the freestyle (halfpipe) Ron Chiodi, 19-year-old phenom Ross Powers and Todd Richards were chosen for the men, and Carabeth Burnside, Barrett Christy, Shannon Dunn and Michele Taggart were selected for the women. Why four? Selection was tight but officials picked women for the extra two team spots (one in GS) because they showed the best promise of medaling in Japan. Gulp.

Wonder woman

Nagano was a zoo. US families got jerked around with tickets – Shannon Dunn's dad

BONNIE ZELLERS SHOWING OFF HER SKILLS.

and brother watched the event with binoculars a half a world away and the sport was being globally ridiculed because Canadian racer Ross Rebagliati won the gold medal. Afterward he tested positive for trace amounts of marijuana. Members of the IOC were lambasting snowboarders for their partying and irresponsibility. This from a committee whose president's wife is said to

have slugged someone in Atlanta during the 1996 summer games.

While the storm raged over Ross, some of the best halfpipe riding was done by the women. If you weren't sticking 720s or huge airs you weren't in contention. Nicola Thost, a German juggernaut, went the biggest with beautiful 720s, ginormous, tweaked straight airs and an good. On her final run she stood at the top of the pipe with a good first-place lead and raised her arms like she was in the pit at a Slayer show. She screamed and hollered and incited the rain-soaked crowd to hoot along with her (albeit in Japanese). She dropped in and did her 720 and McTwist. She bobbled coming off a wall (a point of contention among lots of armchair judges) and with the point deduction she wound up with a bronze medal. When it came time for her post-game interview I figured she'd be disappointed some other lady went home with the precious first-place paper-weight. Instead she said it was the most fun she had ever had in a contest. She congratulated Nicola on the gold, Stine on the silver, and screamed once again, "This is the best!" Well, she certainly made it seem that way, yeah.

"The riding was nuts!" Kennedy

There will be more Olympics for snow-boarding's men and women, now openly vying to outspin and outride each other in the halfpipe and on the race course. But the XVIIIth Winter Olympics, with its historic inclusion of the young but fastest-growing winter sport, belonged more than ever to the women who abandoned traditional roles in traditional sports and dominated on their own terms. They'll remain legends for the speed of their advance and how they inspire.

I'm sure the likes of Tina, Shannon, Michele and even my camper friend Paige could turn out to be mothers of a different sort, who, when their daughters phone in to share some dangerous new experience, will shrug and say, "Whatever it is, hope you had fun."

NICOLA THOST, GOLD MEDAL HALFPIPE, OLYMPICS 1998.

unshakable determination. Stine Brun Kjeldaas, a Norwegian Wonder Woman with long black hair and a big smile, also threw down a staggering consistency and variety of moves.

The most inspirational vixen, I felt, was a certain American filly practically in tears from laughing. To me, Shannon Dunn personified why snowboarding is what it is – why it feels so

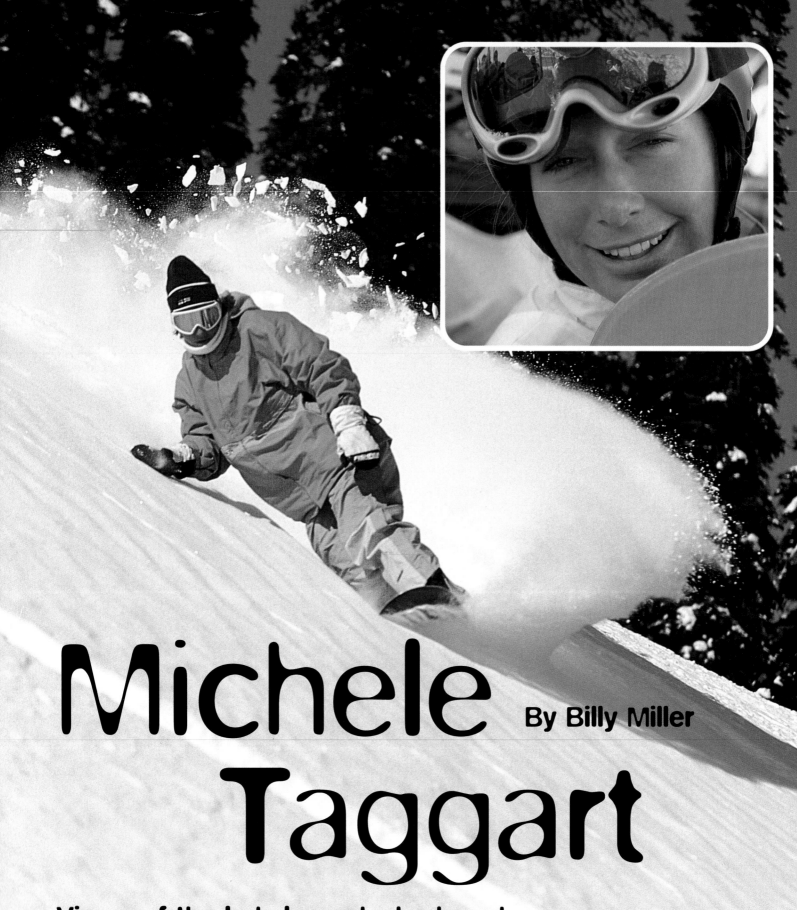

Michele

By Billy Miller

Taggart

**Views of the lady legend who has done more
and won more than most riders dream of.**

anything you can do, 27-year-old Michele Taggart can do better. Taggart is a staggering five-time winner of the Overall title and the winningest female rider in competition history in both Alpine and freestyle, before dropping racing to concentrate on halfpipe and freeriding. She held the US Halfpipe title from 1990-1995, except 1992, and in 1998 became the World Halfpipe Champion after recovering from a broken leg. Despite a hectic competition schedule Taggart maintains a hardcharging freeride presence in both films and photos.

But in person Michele is no aggro overachiever, a easygoing, sweet soul, cracking up more often than not. Her success is born of natural super athlete powers and a keen competitive mind. Always restless for a new challenge, a ball of energy rarely contained, she continues setting the pace in pro snowboarding, and that doesn't mean for women only. One conversation comes from 1995 when Taggart was on top of both race and halfpipe standings, the other after her busy post-injury 1998, which included nabbing a spot on the first US dream team of Olympic snowboarders.

1998

Give us some background on how you started riding?

I skied for a long time. When I was going to high school in Salem [Oregon] there were six or seven guys who would drive to Mt. Bachelor every weekend to snowboard. My brother Dennis was one of them, Rob Morrow, Jake Hauswirth, Chris Sammee ... I was still skiing, thinking, "what are those guys doing?" They spent their day rolling around the wet Oregon snow in wetsuits. The boards had no metal edges and full swallowtails. Rob had this thing where he took the shell of a boot and screwed it onto the board. They just did wacky things.

What year was that?

1987. Then about a year later they got to the point where they could actually make turns. I tried it and just remember wallowing in snow – waist-deep powder. By the end of the day I could make it down the hill so I came in thinking, "this is so exciting!"

How did you start competing?

My third time riding we went to Hoodoo Ski Bowl and I saw Rob Morrow's sister and his girlfriend at the time in the parking lot and they were like, "You've got to enter this contest!" They were having a contest on the hill and needed five riders to have a girls' division but they only had four. I was like, "I can't, I don't know how to snowboard." But they talked me into it.

How'd you do?

I won [laughing]! I seriously didn't know what I was doing, but it was really fun. I think what brought me into doing more is just how fun it was.

What year was that?

That was in 1988, I was in high school. I went to my first World Cup in Breckenridge that year. It was my 10th time snowboarding, I was just freaking out seeing all the same people you see in the magazines.

And now you're one of them.

It's so funny. In the 1989 season they had the Canadian Op Series and basically everyone who entered won [laughs]. We were laughing in the starting gate going, "Three, two, one, cashing in!" Around every gate, "Cha-ching!" We were cracking up about how there we were doing something we love, only 18 and every gate you turn around was money [laughs].

How does that compare with now?

Totally different. But still fun. All of snowboarding has changed. When we first started, anytime you'd see another snowboarder – on the lift, on the run it didn't matter who it was, it was like, "Snowboard with me!" It's not like that anymore.

1995

You and Bertrand Denervaud seem to be the only ones trying.

The overall is something you can train for because you end up going conservative, trying to get the points in every event. There're not that many people who do all three events. Most people cut one thing. I think respect is due to the people trying.

You respect the ones who try how do you feel about the ones who don't?

I think that's cool, too. When I was in school doing team sports, I could never decide, either. I'd go from one [sport] practice to another practice to another ...

1998

In 1996 you stopped racing Alpine?

Stopped doing Alpine and broke my leg. It was actually kind of a good thing. After I quit racing I was super stoked on just freeriding and getting that style back. Then I broke my leg at the weirdest time – after 10 days in Switzerland riding the best snow – I'd just switched from Burton to Salomon, I was all revved up for the season, just having the best time of my life.

You had to miss the first Grand Prix Olympic qualifiers.

But breaking my leg was the best thing that could've happened. After that I had to sit on the couch, still fired up to ride and see how I could do, so when I came back I really wanted to step up.

1995

What do you have planned for the future?

I want to do a lot more freeriding. The last few years I concentrated on racing, and maybe my freestyle went down a little bit. I want to concentrate on freeriding and halfpipe. I just want to go out and ride some mountains

What would you like to see happen in competition?

Well-organized events, perfect facilities, lots of sponsor money, and lots of snow dumping all over the world.

1998

Detail some of your Olympic experience.

Nobody was hiking the pipe and for me that's one of the funnest parts of riding pipe, is walking up the side, cheering on your buddies, "Go bigger!" dropping in together and trying a trick. At the top you had to funnel into a big corrale with people guarding the gate. I almost got a negative taste of everything. At the [US Team] press conference in Mammoth, I got kind of bitter all of a sudden. There was this guy saying, "This is going to change your life!" I was offended – everything changes my life. This isn't why I snowboard, to get yelled at.

Was it all negative?

Oh no. What I really enjoyed was meeting the other athletes talking with them about their life. They're so dedicated to their sports. It was just so hectic, competing in the midst of all these crazy media people, who half the time have their story in mind they want to

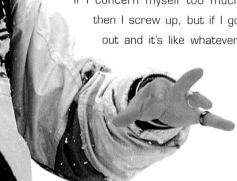

write anyway. They already know how they want to portray snowboarding.

What effect do you think the Olympics had on snowboarding?

I'm just afraid everyone's going to be focused on results and contests, and so much of snowboarding has nothing to do with that. I hope people keep riding to ride, as opposed to riding to win. I don't ride to win, I like to ride to ride. I enjoy what I do and not because it's in the Olympics. For Joe Blow on the street it's like, "Oh wow you're in the Olympics, now you're cool. Not "now I'm cool," now you realize I enjoy what I do. I think in the next four years it's going to get really, really serious ... There's kids that are so good and they're just going to be training their butts off. Maybe they won't know how to ride but they're going to be damn good at halfpipe.

1995

What inspires or influences you?

Hmmm. That's hard to say. I guess the fun factor. I've never done anything I didn't enjoy. I've always loved what I was doing, so I just put all my energy into it. I'm always thinking that way. I don't think about the points at all. You can always have a shitty race, a good race, you just have to go out and have fun. I'm still going into next year with the same attitude – because it's fun, because it's there.

Do you find it hard to maintain such a positive attitude?

If I concern myself too much then I screw up, but if I go out and it's like whatever,

just do my best, it works out. One thing I always think about is trying to put all my energy in just one area. It's hard – if I did that I wonder what I'd be able to accomplish. But if I did, I'd probably get bored and be out of it in a year. If you are doing what you love to do, it is pretty darn easy. And how could anyone not love snowboarding?

1998

What did you do after the Olympics?

This year's season was pretty interesting. I was dedicated to doing contests the first half of the year and the next half, freeriding and photo shoots. It broke up the season. Next year I'll continue concentrating on the two, doing the big events and more photo shoots if possible. See how that goes for the next couple years then see how it's going for the 2002 Olympics.

Want to give it another shot?

Maybe I'll jump in the halfpipe more seriously then and see how competitive I am at

the time. I'd like to remove myself from competing a bit and see how well I'm doing. If I'm still up there, I'll give it 110 percent. It's still fun but I really want to get away from all that and concentrate on freeriding.

Is it harder to get what sponsors want with freeriding?

I got juked on the weather a few times but it happens. I feel I push my level of snowboarding when I'm out taking photos. Just knowing I need to do more I'll practice to learn new tricks so there's new progress to show on film. Right now I don't want to kick back on what I've done in the past.

Your whole family travels.

We've always traveled ever since I was a kid. I'm still way into traveling, but sometime at the end of the season, it's nice to be home. It's ideal to have Mt. Hood, and when it's raining I can go home. I love what I'm doing – why not continue?

"If you're going to do what you love to do, it's pretty darn easy. And how could anyone not love snowboarding?"
Michele Taggart.

Results

• Overall World Cup Tour Champion 1995

• World Giant Slalom Champion 1995

• 1993 Overall World Champion halfpipe, GS, and slalom (held every two years)

• Holder of all Overall titles 1990-'95

• Second place 1996 Quiksilver Cup (boardercross and surfing)

• Five-time US Halfpipe Title holder, 1990, '91, '93, '94, '95

• 1998 ISF World Halfpipe Champion

Snowboarding's timeline

A countdown through 78 years of snow-sliding history

1910 – 'Bunkering' is all the rage: the sport of sliding down a hill standing on sleds made from the wooden slats of a barrel, nailed together, with a rope handle tied to the front.

1965 – Sherman Poppen invents the Snurfer by bolting two skis together.

1970 – Inspired by sliding on trays, East Coast surfer Dimitrije Milovich starts developing snowboards based on surfboard design.

1969–72 – Bob Webber obtains a patent for his early 'Skiboard' design.

1977 – Jake Burton Carpenter moves to Vermont and designs the prototypes for what will become Burton Snowboards.

1978 – Chuck Barfoot develops a fiberglass prototype snowboard, and he and Bob Webber take it out to Utah for a test run.

1979 – At the annual Snurfer contest Snurfer pro Paul Graves puts on a freestyle demo and wows the crowd. At the same event Jake Burton Carpenter tries to enter on his own equipment.

Mark Anolik discovers the Tahoe City Halfpipe while nosing around behind the Tahoe City dump. This becomes known as the world's first snowboard halfpipe.

1979–80 – *Skateboarder* and *Action Now* magazines both print early features on the rising sport of snowboarding. *Powder* features the first equipment review.

1981 – Modern competitive snowboarding begins with a small contest held in April at Ski Cooper in Leadville, Colorado.

1982 – Paul Graves organizes the National Snowsurfing Championships, held at Suicide Six Ski Area in Woodstock, Vermont, featuring a slalom and downhill. This is the first time riders from all over the country compete against each other and marks the last time Snurfers and snowboards race together.

1983 – Jake Burton Carpenter puts on the National Snowboarding Championships in the spring at Snow Valley, Vermont. Tom Sims attends, then goes home and holds the inaugural World Snowboarding Championships at Soda Springs Ski Bowl in the Lake Tahoe area – the first contest to have a halfpipe event.

1985 – Mount Baker hosts the first Mount Baker Legendary Banked Slalom. It becomes a competitive mainstay. Tom Sims wins.

Absolutely Radical, the first exclusively snowboarding magazine appears. It later becomes *International Snowboard Magazine*.

Snowboarding makes its big-screen debut in *A View to a Kill*, featuring Tom Sims and Steve Link doubling for Roger Moore.

1986 – Europeans begin to organize regional events, such as the Swiss Championships in Saint Moritz.

Apocalypse Snow, the first snowboarding film of note is made by Regis Roland, one of France's snowboarding pioneers.

During this winter, Stratton Mountain in Vermont becomes the first resort to offer organized snowboarding instruction.

Tom Burt, Jim Zellers and Bonnie Zellers (then Leary) mark the beginning of professional freeriding by scheduling photo shoots and riding 'extreme' terrain for Avalanche Snowboards.

1987 – After the second Breckenridge Worlds in March, Paul Alden and a collection of riders and manufacturers form the North American Snowboard Association (NASA). The acronym is later changed to NASBA because the other one is already taken.

A host of early snowboarders pen the first Professional Ski Instructors of America manual for snowboard instructors.

TransWorld SNOWboarding Magazine publishes its first issue.

1987–88 – The first World Cup is held throughout the season with two events in Europe and two in the United States. The circuit also introduces major corporate sponsorship into the competitive arena.

1988 – Surfer Publications joins in with *Snowboarder Magazine*.

United States Amateur Snowboarding Association (USASA) is incorporated – aided by a $500 donation from *TransWorld SNOWboarding Magazine*. USASA is the first governing body exclusively for competitive amateur snowboarding.

1989 – Most of the major ski resorts that have previously resisted snowboarding succumb, such as Squaw Valley, California; Mammoth Mountain, California; Vail, Colorado; Sun Valley, Idaho and Snowbird, Utah–all in time for the coming winter.

The first National Collegiate championships are held at Stratton Mountain, Vermont.

1990 – Jake Burton Carpenter buys the patent for the 'Skiboard' from designer Bob Webber. Burton's lawyers send out a letter asking for three per cent of everyone's total sales. The industry dares Burton to enforce the patent, and Jake backs off.

The USASA holds its premier national championship in February at Snow Valley, California.

1990 – In June, Breckenridge Ski Corp announces plans to house the Snowboarding Hall of Fame, with artifacts from the sport's not-so-distant past.

Vail Ski Resort tries a new approach by developing an in-bounds obstacle area called a 'snowboard park'. The area is intended to cater to a growing snowboard market and other resorts quickly follow suit.

1995 – Liability wavers are proved to work. California Superior Court rules that Burton

The International Snowboard Federation forms after the collapse of the North American Professional Snowboard Association.

1991 – The Victoria World Cup Japan is held at Rusutsu Resort on Japan's north island. With over $1 million spent on the contest, it's the richest event thus far.

1992 – The United States Ski Association decides to become involved with snowboarding. The USSA tries to merge with the USASA. Negotiations fail.

1993 – In January the International Snowboard Federation holds its first official Snowboard World Championships in Ischgl, Austria. Americans Kevin Delaney and Michele Taggart win the combined titles.

The Federation International du Ski (FIS), the international body for skiing, votes to recognize snowboarding at its June meeting.

Snowboarder TV goes on the air at ESPN with host 'GT', Greg Tomlinson. It is the sport's first serialized television show.

Matt Goodwill and Greta Gaines win the men's and women's titles at the first-ever World Extreme Snowboard Championships in Valdez, Alaska.

1994 – At the Lillehammer, Norway Olympics it is hoped that snowboarding will be performed as a 'cultural exhibition' by the host country. The FIS gets wind of the performance and forces its cancellation.

The first Amateur World Championships are held in Slovenia.

May 6. Ride Snowboards becomes the first snowboard company to go public on the NASDAQ stock exchange. The original 500,000 units sell out in the first two weeks and another 75,000 units are released. Those who buy early rake in the profit as Ride stock grows in value by nearly six times.

June. At its national congress in Rio De Janeiro, the FIS membership votes to include snowboarding as a discipline under its jurisdiction.

July. ISF president Ted Martin writes a letter asking the IOC to recognize the ISF as the governing body of international snowboarding. In a three-sentence reply, the ISF is told to talk to the FIS about getting ISF athletes in the Olympics because 'FIS governs that discipline.' Martin now works for the FIS.

August. Burton Snowboards releases the first CD-ROM interactive catalog, taking snowboarding into the computer age.

Heckler magazine, based in Sacramento, California, becomes the first snowboard magazine to publish on the Internet World Wide Web (http://heckler.com/heckler/).

Snowboards and Ski Shop Santa Cruz are not responsible for the death of a snowboarder, because he signed the liability release when he purchased the board.

At the International Olympic Committee meeting in Karuizawa, Japan on December 5, organizers of the 1998 Nagano Winter Olympics announce that snowboarding will be included in their Games, with men's and women's giant slalom and halfpipe getting the nod.

1996 – The run is over. The Japanese market is flooded with an estimated 800,000 boards in inventory. The world market is also flooded with equipment, accelerating pressure on the industry to consolidate. On a good note, the overall snowboard population continues to grow at an estimated 20-30 per cent per year around the globe.

1997 – Snowboarding continues to be the fastest-growing winter sport in the US as the population nears four million. The National Sporting Goods Association shows the snowboard population to be 3.7 million, up 32.5 per cent from the previous year.

The USSA is panned by the snowboarding community for its slow organization of an acceptable Olympic team qualifier and for accepting some reported millions from Jim Hensen Productions to make its Muppet character, Animal, the team's official mascot.

Resorts are deemed not responsible for snowboard-park injuries. In September, a jury does not impose liability on Sierra-At-Tahoe Ski Resort for injuries suffered by a rider in the resort's snowboard park. The case is significant because it sends a message to both resorts and riders. That snowboarders are likely to be held personally responsible for their park-related injuries.

Susanna Howe's *Sick: A Cultural History of Snowboarding* is the first book to take a serious, historical look at snowboarding.

1998 – After hotly contested qualifiers and political battles the world over, snowboarding finally makes a much-heralded Olympic debut at the XVIII Games in Nagano, Japan. Canadian Ross Rebagliati and Frenchwoman Karine Ruby win the first gold medals in the Giant Slalom. Two days later Rebagliati is stripped of his medal in a 12-13 vote for testing positive for marijuana. Rebagliati claims he inhaled smoke "second-hand" at a party. After much media hype and speculation the world over, Rebagliati is given back his medal, with the IOC pledging to adopt a uniform marijuana policy. Two other athletes are identified as testing positive for the drug during the Games, but their names and sports are not revealed. Gian Simmen from Switzerland and Nicola Thost from Germany take the golds in the first-ever Olympic snowboard halfpipe. Animal is scarcely heard from.

Everyone who owns a snowboard would still rather go ride powder and wishes they could look as stylish as Craig Kelly.